Advance Praise for *Great on the Job*

"A master class in workplace success—*Great on the Job* is a must-read for anyone looking to get ahead in their career."
—Keith Ferrazzi, *New York Times* bestselling author of *Who's Got Your Back* and *Never Eat Alone*

"*Great on the Job* is practical, clever, and thoughtfully presented. My professional life has given me a bird's-eye view of the negative effects of underhoned 'soft skills.' In *Great on the Job*, Jodi Glickman shows a rich understanding of how basic communications can make or break business relationships and careers. This book, with its wide variety of common scenarios and suggestions, is a must-have resource for professionals who understand that success always depends upon quality communications."
—Joseph Thomas, dean of the Johnson Graduate School of Management, Cornell University

"If you want to improve your communication skills, this is the book for you. Jodi Glickman tackles the most common difficulties in business communication with real-world examples of what to say—and how to say it. Her three-step models are highly efficient tools that improve effectiveness, inspire confidence, and enhance careers."
—William J. White, former chairman and CEO of Bell & Howell

"*Great on the Job* is the *answer* to building credibility at work. Rather than offering up generalized advice, this engaging guidebook delivers precise mechanics for communicating persuasively. Glickman, a trusted adviser and communications expert, imparts her own hard-won business lessons to help you maneuver through those sticky, hard-to-navigate situations with savvy."
—Selena Rezvani, columnist for *The Washington Post* and author of *The Next Generation of Women Leaders: What You Need to Lead but Won't Learn in Business School*

"We live in a technology-driven world that often makes interpersonal communication unnecessary. Yet if you want to inspire people and

experience real success in your career, you have to step away from the computer and learn to lead face-to-face. What I love about Jodi's approach is that she believes—as I do—that communication is not a 'soft' skill at all. It's a hard skill that can be taught, and she's the expert to do it."

—Emily Bennington, author of *Effective Immediately: How to Fit In, Stand Out, and Move Up at Your First Real Job*

"Jodi Glickman leverages her success in business school, finance, and entrepreneurship to teach readers, step by step, how to achieve desired results in any workplace conversation. *Great on the Job*'s approach of turning effective communication from a soft skill that you either have or you don't to a hard skill that can be practiced and mastered by anyone is sheer brilliance."

—Alexandra Levit, nationally syndicated business columnist and author of *New Job, New You*

"Jodi Glickman is an outrageously good communicator, and in *Great on the Job* she generously shares all of her tips, tricks, secrets, and scripts. Every professional—but particularly those just starting out—will benefit from her step-by-step approach to saying the right things at the right time in the right way. I highly recommend this book."

—Lindsey Pollak, author of *Getting from College to Career: 90 Things to Do Before You Join the Real World*

"In today's competitive business environment, being 'good' at work is simply not enough. To stand out from the crowd, you must have the tools to effectively communicate, collaborate, receive feedback, and highlight success. Thanks to Jodi and *Great on the Job,* the art and science behind expert communication is no longer a mystery. This is a book that needed to be written—the top-notch advice, tactical strategies, and real-world examples are a blueprint for how to master workplace communication. Don't miss a great opportunity in your career because of a conversation that could have gone better or a question you should have thought to ask—do yourself a favor and read this book now."

—Cari Sommer, cofounder of Urban Interns

GREAT

what to say

ON THE

how to say it

JOB

the secrets of getting ahead

Jodi Glickman

 ST. MARTIN'S GRIFFIN  New York

The case studies described in this book are based on true events, but names of individuals and organizations are either fictitious or disguised.

GREAT ON THE JOB. Copyright © 2011 by Jodi Glickman. All rights reserved. Printed in the United States of America. For information, address St. Martin's Press, 175 Fifth Avenue, New York, N.Y. 10010.

www.stmartins.com

Design by Patrice Sheridan

LIBRARY OF CONGRESS CATALOGING-IN-PUBLICATION DATA

Glickman, Jodi.
    Great on the job : what to say, how to say it : the secrets of getting ahead / Jodi Glickman. — 1st ed.
        p. cm.
    ISBN 978-0-312-64146-7
    1. Business communication.   2. Success in business.   I. Great on the Job (Firm).   II. Title.
    HF5718.G55 2011
    650.1—dc22

2011002713

First Edition: May 2011

10 9 8 7 6 5 4 3 2 1

for my dad

Richard S. Glickman

---

in loving memory of your

brilliant mind, outsized heart

& irreverent spirit.

---

i miss you.

Contents

Contents

Introduction

In 2009, Warren Buffett and Bill Gates addressed an audience of Columbia Business School students. Buffett was asked the one piece of advice he'd give to new graduates. To much applause and laughter Buffet responded:

> Right now, I would pay a hundred thousand dollars for ten percent of the future earnings of any of you. If that's true, you're a million-dollar asset right now. You could improve on that, many of you, and I certainly could have when I got out, just in terms of learning communication skills.
>
> *It's not something that's taught* . . . but if you improve your value fifty percent by having better communication skills, it's another five hundred thousand dollars in terms of capital value. See me after the class and I'll pay you one hundred and fifty thousand.

Buffet hit the nail on the head: communication skills are important and they're not taught. The vast majority of

How many courses have you taken on how you talk with an employee you're firing? Or, how do you talk with the person who comes to your office late at night to tell you that her daughter is sick and she might not be able to come in the following day?

As managers and leaders of people, those are the kinds of questions that one deals with probably eighty percent of the time.

—*Eduardo Castro-Wright, Vice Chairman, Wal-Mart*

professionals rely on experiential learning when it comes to daily conversation and the critical skills and strategies necessary to "make it" on the job.

How many of you have taken a formal course on how to ask for help? How about how to answer a question you don't know the answer to? How many of you have ever had anyone cover the topic of raising a red flag when a problem arises or how to effectively ask for feedback from your supervisor?

Giving effective feedback—that's covered ad nauseam. Public speaking, ditto. Interacting with a client? That's covered too, but typically within the context of having a firm handshake, good eye contact, or displaying confidence. But how helpful is it when someone tells you to "be confident" or "think outside the box"? What does that mean and how do I implement it?

Traditionally, people either were good communicators, or not. They either "had it," or they didn't. They connected with people and moved ahead, or didn't, and perhaps wondered why.

Moreover, when you had a workplace question, you typically asked a friend, colleague, spouse, or parent. The problem with this approach was twofold. First, there was limited perspective among those around you—how did you know that the friend, colleague, spouse, or parent you asked actually had a good answer? Second, the execution wasn't guaranteed—who's to say that even if and when you got good advice, you actually knew how to implement it?

That's all about to change.

Communication is the only task you cannot delegate.

—ROBERTO GOIZUETA, FORMER CEO, COCA-COLA

In 2008, I launched the consulting firm Great on the Job (GOTJ) to meet an unmet and, as of then, unidentified need in the marketplace: to teach people how to talk to one another at work, every day, in every situation, in all stages of their careers, whether they are on the top of their game or have no idea what the #$% is going on.

Great on the Job offers simple action strategies (usually 1-2-3–step processes) and example language to give people the tools they need to communicate effectively, strategically, and persuasively on the job—and to convey competence, confidence, and professionalism in *all* workplace encounters.

The Great on the Job methodology is proven, easy to implement, and doesn't require any homework. The roster of corporate and business-school clients who've hired Great on the Job to train their employees and students reads as a who's who of the best and the brightest: Harvard Business School, Wharton School, NYU Stern School of Business, Johnson School at Cornell, Kellogg School of Management, Citigroup, Bank of America/Merrill Lynch, and much of Wall Street. My clients couldn't be more satisfied. They find the skills Great on the Job teaches timely, urgent, and extremely impactful, and I consistently receive over 90 percent approval ratings for my presentations on workplace effectiveness.

Why Now?

People aren't required to speak live anymore. They can send an e-mail, leave a voice mail, send a text or instant message, get their news via Twitter, and connect with friends on Facebook.

But business still is—and will always be—a personal thing. Dynamic and honed interpersonal skills are *the* keys to success in the workplace. Across industries, across professions, across the board from the rank and file to the executive suite, communication and relationship skills are key.

The art of live communication and relationship building remains critically important no matter what industry you work in. In today's global economy, it's typically not the smartest, hardest-working, or most technically savvy who succeed. Even those who have complete mastery over the technical aspects of their jobs need to communicate and relate to others effectively and strategically to earn the respect, trust, and admiration of their colleagues—indeed, in order to succeed. The ability to communicate well is often *the* most important precursor to success in the workplace.

And while opportunities to engage in real one-on-one dialogue are dwindling, those we do engage in it become all the more important. With fewer opportunities to practice, an entire generation of young professionals is growing up rudderless in knowing how and when to speak. When they do speak up, the result is oftentimes horrifying.

And so, there is Great on the Job. Having taught thousands of undergraduates and business-school students, Wall Street analysts and associates,

Great on the Job gives readers foolproof strategies to:

- *Communicate effectively, strategically, and persuasively on the job*
- *Convey competence, confidence, and professionalism in all workplace encounters*

and young professionals in nonprofits and corporate America how to communicate effectively and strategically, I am sharing my simple yet groundbreaking methods with you, the reader, in hopes of revolutionizing how we relate to, and interact with, one another in the workplace.

My goal is to make you a better communicator, a more productive employee, and a happier person—because you'll do better at your job and you'll see positive results in all that you do.

How Does It Work?

Great on the Job is built on the premise that the art of communication can be translated into a science. Great on the Job uses micro-analysis to create a methodology that can be learned, practiced, and implemented immediately. There is a formula, a road map, a template—a tangible, practical guide that can get you from point A to point B in your next workplace conversation. Put another way, GOTJ takes a "soft" skill and turns it into a "hard" or technical skill.

Here's how GOTJ works: I take you through hundreds of conversations, soup to nuts, and give you the following:

1. *Situational Analysis:* Working America has many similarities across industries and across professions, in firms that provide services or produce products, and among employees who work for a CEO, Uncle Sam, or an executive director. People often work in teams—everyone has a boss, colleagues, superiors, or subordinates. You have deliverables, deadlines, and tasks at hand. Most of these situations can be examined collectively to give clues on how to handle them individually and effectively, no matter the specifics. In effect, Joe from accounting or Jane from marketing had a similar issue, and here's what happened. . . .

2. *Action Strategy:* Just as professional athletes analyze game film frame by frame, Great on the Job breaks down its strategies to the smallest of parts to make them digestible, easy to learn, understand, and teach. GOTJ strategies are tactical, practical, and easy to implement. There's no theory here. No high-level concepts or homework assignments. These are just 1-2-3–step strategies that you can take with you and use tomorrow. They are basic, "in the weeds" strategies that can be used immediately.

3. *Example Language:* GOTJ "example language" charts give readers a selection of phrases that can be used for each step of an action strategy. These charts aren't meant as scripts to be memorized. Rather, they give you ideas of language

that can be used to express each idea professionally—that is, effectively, strategically, and/or persuasively. Think of the example language charts as jumping-off points to get you started thinking about what to say and how to say it. You can then modify and tweak your phrases to work best for you.

4. *Troubleshooting:* But what about _____? Yes, there will always be exceptions to every rule, and no strategy will work 100 percent of the time. Troubleshooting answers some common questions and objections to the strategies and gives you tools to work with when a specific strategy isn't a perfect fit for your particular situation.

Most important of all, will GOTJ work for you? The answer is yes. Immediately upon reading a chapter, you should have all the guidance you need to go ahead and put these action strategies and example language into practice tomorrow. If you don't feel that way, please e-mail me at jodi@greatonthejob.com and push back—tell me where I'm coming up short. That's how I continually improve upon and hone this product.

Who Am I?

Finally, before we jump in, you probably want to know a little bit about me and how I came to be Great on the Job. For those of you taking nontraditional career paths, take comfort in knowing that I wore many hats before becoming an entrepreneur and communication expert. I've always been the latter, I just never knew it.

I am a Peace Corps volunteer turned investment banker turned communication expert. All of my professional success, in government, nonprofit, finance, and corporate America, has been due to my interpersonal skills. As much as I'd like to describe myself as a finance whiz or a policy wonk, I am by no means either. I was always smart enough to get in the door, and I'm an extremely hard worker. But at the end of the day, just as some people get by on their looks, for me it was always my ability to relate to, and connect with, people.

It took a round-the-clock job and an extraordinarily observant husband to identify my true gift. My husband and I are like peanut butter and jelly—our skill sets are almost completely inversely aligned. He is creative, insightful, and an extraordinary listener. I am analytical, linear, and a great talker.

Over the years, Eric spent many hours listening to me on conference calls, leaving voice mails, and just generally working my butt off on a 24-7 Wall Street schedule. Eric noticed immediately that we handled ourselves differently in professional situations. He began asking questions and making observations, such as "I would never have thought to ask for help that way" or "I don't know how to end a conversation like you do—how do you do it?" or "That was a brilliant way to tell everyone you had just screwed up."

Eric started taking notes. In 2007, he e-mailed me a business plan outlining the basics of Great on the Job. I thought he was crazy. Eric persisted and we eventually started working on a project to "reverse engineer" the daily conversations that make up a typical workday. Great on the Job, the consulting business, was born shortly thereafter, and ever since then we have been diagramming and road-mapping the most frequent and repetitive conversations in the workplace.

Some anecdotal evidence also supports my uncanny ability to communicate effectively no matter the situation:

- I was hired as an investment-banking associate at Goldman Sachs in October 2001 with arguably shaky finance skills (I got a C+ in finance class).
- I landed a summer internship in business school with Exxon Mobil's Treasury Department without interviewing—a casual conversation with the treasurer of Exxon Mobil Chemical resulted in a job offer. Ten of my classmates had gone through the formal interview process.
- I applied for a job at the U.S. EPA when they weren't readily accepting applicants. I assured my future boss on the phone that if she met me, she would hire me. I flew to Washington, D.C., to interview and was offered the job.
- I was told I had the best interview for a job even though the hiring committee acknowledged I was the least qualified of all the candidates.
- On a 360-degree performance review at Goldman Sachs, I had the highest ranking for communication skills among the associate classes (three hundred–plus people).
- I applied to the Johnson Graduate School of Management (JGSM) in hopes of securing a Park Leadership

Fellowship, a $72,000 scholarship for two years. I was admitted to JGSM but was not offered the fellowship. I called the director of the program to lobby for the award. The next day, the program director called me to personally offer me the fellowship. I received my MBA (for free) as a Park Leadership Fellow in 2002.

And finally, since 2008, I've been spending every minute of every day thinking about this stuff—reverse engineering the daily conversations in the workplace by breaking them down into their smallest parts, studying and analyzing what works and what doesn't, and then coming up with strategies to improve upon each and every one. I've been talking with and training thousands of people across corporate America and asking myself the questions (or having them asked of me) "What do you do when . . . ?" and "How should I handle this conversation?"

In the same way that Bill Gates had ten thousand expert hours of software programming under his belt when he launched Microsoft (at the ripe old age of twenty-one), by the time you're reading this book, I'm at about seven thousand expert hours and counting. Let's jump in and get started.

G*I*F*T

You will see four key themes throughout *Great on the Job*. Understand these concepts from the outset and you'll be ready to tackle the practical, tactical, use-'em-right-away strategies that start in the next chapter.

Generosity, *Initiative*, *Forward Momentum*, and *Transparency*: they are the GIFT of *Great on the Job* and they will come into play repeatedly as you move through the book. They are the only high-level concepts I'll cover, but they're worth our while for a quick discussion. Let's take a look at each one separately.

Generosity

I read something early on that you can accomplish almost anything in life if you do not care who takes credit for it.

—EDUARDO CASTRO-WRIGHT, VICE CHAIRMAN, WAL-MART

When you think about critical business skills, generosity is not one that typically first comes to mind. Drive, ambition, motivation, leadership, vision—those are some of the characteristics you likely think of first.

However, generosity is a key component of effective communication. It doesn't matter how much drive or motivation you've got, if you don't share information with team members openly, share credit with colleagues readily, put others' agendas and schedules ahead of your own when necessary, and help your colleagues, then you're missing a critical business skill.

Being generous shows you are a good team player, it makes people like you, it creates goodwill with people you work for and with people who work for you. It's the basic law of karma—the more good you put out into the world, the more that comes back to you.

Dirk made the first [shot] and we missed the second [shot].

—Mark Cuban, owner, Dallas Mavericks,
referring to star player Dirk Nowitzki

Mark Cuban, owner of the Dallas Mavericks, was asked by a reporter about team captain Dirk Nowitzki's missed game-tying free-throw shot. Cuban pointed out that Nowitzki made the first shot but conceded that "we" (the team) missed the second one.

Giving individual praise for success and assuming collective responsibility for failure is inherently generous, and distinctively subtle. Cuban recognized an opportunity in the situation—a simple *we* instead of a *he* reminded fans that basketball is indeed a team sport. Cuban shared credit instead of assigning blame and propped up his star player to engender goodwill.

The next time you or someone on your team "misses the boat" on an assignment or fails to deliver on time, think about Mark Cuban's comments. Generosity is a powerful tool—the more you do to make someone else's life better, the more you'll do for yourself in advancing your own career.

You will see the theme of generosity in the following chapters:

- Chapter 1, "Master the Hello and Good-Bye" (page 3): being considerate of people's time (e.g., asking someone at the outset of a conversation if it's a good time to talk).
- Chapter 2, "The Foolproof Download" (page 19): leading with the punch line—sharing information readily and up front, not making people wait for or guess at the meaning or the important parts of your conversation.
- Chapter 3, "Be Strategically Proactive" (page 43): assisting others—going above and beyond the call of duty or digging in and getting your hands dirty even though you're not required to do so.
- Chapter 6, "Ask for Feedback" (page 117): scheduling the conversation around the other person's calendar and providing specific areas of performance you are looking for feedback on (versus the vague "How am I doing?"—which creates work for the other person).
- Chapter 8, "Raise a Red Flag" (page 165): highlighting problems early, coming armed with solutions.

- Chapter 9, "Manage a Crisis" (page 183): proactively coming up with solutions to problems.

Initiative

A lot of people in business say they have twenty years' experience, when in fact all they really have is one year's experience, repeated twenty times.

—HUGH MACLEOD, AUTHOR OF *IGNORE EVERYBODY*

Taking initiative and being proactive are hardly novel concepts in the business world. Everyone knows that being proactive is an essential skill in business—you've got to make things happen *for* you instead of waiting for them to happen *to* you. The number one habit in Stephen Covey's world-renowned *The 7 Habits of Highly Effective People* is "Be Proactive."

The question, then, isn't "Should I take initiative?" It's "How do I take initiative?" How can I be *strategically* proactive? How can I be helpful when I'm not sure how or where to start? How can I take an active role in shaping my assignments, working with good people, or contributing to high-profile or high-impact teams? And if I can't do any of those in the near term, how can I be helpful in assisting others with less exciting work now in hope of making more plum assignments come my way over the longer term?

Taking the concept one step further, ask yourself

how you can be proactive without creating more work for others. You'll see me argue in chapter 3, "Be Strategically Proactive," that the question "How can I help?" isn't actually all that helpful. It creates work for someone else by requiring them to come up with something for you to do.

The *GOTJ* approach gives people choices so that others can respond to your specific offers of help without having to dream up answers on their own. Think of it as the difference between taking an essay and a multiple-choice test in college. For most people, having a menu of options from which to choose is preferable to having to come up with an idea from a blank page.

Being strategically proactive also means moving your career forward by engaging in meaningful and productive work that contributes to the greater good. The *GOTJ* strategy for doing that is called the LEARN strategy. L★E★A★R★N stands for:

- **L**earn
- **E**xcel
- **A**ssist
- **R**edirect
- **N**etwork

Each of these goals can be a driving factor when you are trying to take initiative and contribute to your organization or advance your career. You can and should be extremely thoughtful, calculated even, in thinking through and creating opportunities for you to learn new skills, excel at things you are good at, assist others, redirect unwanted work, and network by creating opportunities to work with people who are highly regarded, well connected, or just great at what they do (so that you can learn from them).

Chapter 3, "Be Strategically Proactive," will discuss this in more detail. In addition, you'll find the concept of taking initiative covered in the following chapters:

- Chapter 2, "The Foolproof Download" (page 19): updating teams regularly, anticipating outstanding issues in advance.
- Chapter 4, "Manage Expectations" (page 69): thinking through your to-do list in advance and knowing your capacity constraints.
- Chapter 5, "Ask for Help" (page 95): asking for the resources and guidance needed to do your work well.
- Chapter 6, "Ask for Feedback" (page 117): soliciting feedback about your performance before it's too late, taking ownership and not assuming its your manager's responsibility to tell you how you're doing.
- Chapter 7, "Answer Questions (You Don't Know the Answers To)" (page 145): going and getting the answer when you don't have it.
- Chapter 8, "Raise a Red Flag" (page 165): alerting teams early to potential problems coming down the pipeline.
- Chapter 10, "Your Personal Elevator Pitch" (page 205): thinking your story through in advance.

Forward Momentum

I've been amazed over the years how relationships that come out of one thing go toward something else. So somebody I might have met through a charity then becomes somebody who knows somebody and it leads to a relationship.

—STEPHEN I. SADOVE, CHAIRMAN AND CEO OF SAKS, INC.

In 2001, as a business-school student at the Johnson School, I had dinner at the home of one of the associate deans of the school. I met Karin Ash that evening and we hit it off. She worked for Cornell University at the time but wasn't in any way affiliated with the business school.

The summer I graduated, Karin joined the Johnson School as director of the Career Management Center. I headed to Wall Street and spent the next four years maintaining semiregular contact with Karin as she continued to send students to Wall Street and I actively recruited at the Johnson School on behalf of Goldman Sachs, my employer at the time.

I was always happy to provide over-the-shoulder advice to students interested in Wall Street, and I cared deeply about recruiting top JGSM talent to my firm. Beyond that, I had no "agenda" in my relationship with Karin.

In 2008, seven years after meeting Karin and two years after leaving Wall Street, I made one of the biggest career changes of my life and decided to launch my own business. My first call was to Karin. I explained the concept behind Great on the Job and asked if I could come up to Ithaca, New York, to do a workshop for the first-year MBAs. Karin gave an enthusiastic yes.

Four weeks later, after my first successful speaking engagement to fifty-five MBA students in Ithaca, I quit my job and officially launched Great on the Job. My relationship with Karin resulted in my first speaking engagement at a major business school, which then provided the credibility I needed to pitch and win my first corporate client. With that, Great on the Job, the business, was born.

Today, my relationship with Karin continues to build and I have received referrals to her colleagues at Harvard, Wharton, Columbia, and NYU, to name a few. Nonetheless, when I met Karin seven years ago, I had no idea I'd ever need or want her help. I didn't have an agenda at the time, but when my career took a 180-degree turn, I had a great ally to reach out to.

Forward momentum is all about nurturing and sustaining relationships. *GOTJ* action strategies are designed to help keep your interactions open-ended and active versus close-ended or one-off. With a minimum amount of work, *GOTJ* strategies encourage and help establish and maintain forward momentum for all future interactions.

Forward momentum will be addressed in the following chapters:

- Chapter 1, "Master the Hello and Good-Bye" (page 3): ending every conversation with momentum for the next conversation.
- Chapter 2, "The Foolproof Download" (page 19): always finishing with follow-up or action items.

- Chapter 3, "Be Strategically Proactive" (page 43): thinking ahead to future assignments and teams.
- Chapter 4, "Manage Expectations" (page 69): thinking about how and when you can get things done and communicating your plan of action going forward.
- Chapter 6, "Ask for Feedback" (page 153): getting input on how to improve next time around.
- Chapter 8, "Raise a Red Flag" (page 165), and Chapter 9, "Manage a Crisis" (page 183): showing how you are moving the ball forward in the face of adversity.
- Chapter 10, "Your Personal Elevator Pitch" (page 205): connecting the dots for people about how your story makes sense or what you hope to do in the future.

Transparency

Just as the *Blue Book* has done wonders for the used-car industry and Bloomberg terminals have brought transparency to the bond market—everyone agrees that information is power. Transparency makes markets more efficient and builds credibility among colleagues. People gravitate toward, and organizations reward, people who tell it like it is and share information readily—not those who hide the truth or hoard information as though it's a precious commodity.

Transparency goes beyond the idea of just being honest and forthright—you should never lie in business. Transparency also includes being up front—being honest about shortfalls or screwups; alerting teams and people to problems early; admitting to not knowing information or sharing what you do know so that others benefit from that information.

Transparency will show up in the following sections of this book:

- Chapter 1, "Master the Hello and Good-Bye" (page 3): stating the purpose of your call.
- Chapter 2, "The Foolproof Download" (page 19): leading with the punch line.
- Chapter 3, "Be Strategically Proactive" (page 43): asking for opportunities to learn a new skill or offering to work on projects where you will excel—being up front about your motives.
- Chapter 5, "Ask for Help" (page 95): not being afraid to admit you don't know how to do something.
- Chapter 7, "Answer Questions (You Don't Know the Answers To)" (page 145): admitting to what you don't know.
- Chapter 8, "Raise a Red Flag" (page 165), and Chapter 9, "Manage a Crisis" (page 183): highlighting problems early.
- Chapter 10, "Your Personal Elevator Pitch" (page 205): knowing and communicating your goals and objectives.

Generosity, Initiative, Forward Momentum, and Transparency—as you read about these concepts, you'll be amazed at how often they show up in your workplace (and personal) interactions. You'll start to listen to people differently and recognize their generosity (or lack thereof) in sharing (or withholding information). Your antennae will go on high alert when a colleague or a subordinate doesn't offer to go find the right answer or a piece of information for you. You'll be amazed at how effective you are by being transparent and using forward momentum to tell someone why you need something or how you're moving the ball forward.

Once you start integrating these four concepts into your everyday actions, you'll find yourself better able to communicate, get people on your side when you need them, and avoid mishaps and miscommunications.

Here we go.

part one

the basics

chapter one

Master the Hello and Good-Bye

Life is a series of hellos and good-byes.

—BILLY JOEL

You'll make an impression just by not taking for granted that [someone] was lying there in a hammock, eating chocolates and reading movie magazines, hoping someone would telephone.

—BARBARA WALTERS

In early 2008, when Great on the Job was nothing more than an idea and a set of PowerPoint slides, I sent my materials to a friend and mentor up at Cornell business school for his review. Clint Sidle, the director of the Park Leadership Fellows Program, had coached me through my transition from Peace Corps volunteer to investment banker years before, and he and I had maintained a close friendship ever since.

Clint thought the slides were great but he had one question early on: The hello and good-bye—did it really need to be taught? My husband, Eric, concurred. He thought it was insulting to people's intelligence to talk to a room full of MBAs and role-play the beginning and end of a phone conversation.

But here's the thing. How many times have you picked up the phone and the person on the other end—your friend, colleague, client, or mother for that matter—launches into a diatribe about something that you're either (a) not interested in, (b) not prepared to discuss, or (c) don't have time to listen to? And you politely (or impolitely) think to yourself, *How do I get off the damn phone?*

Too many of us have been on the receiving end of a call when we weren't awarded the common courtesy of being asked if we had a moment to speak. Unfortunately, we found ourselves wondering how to end the call or thinking about the hundreds of other things on our to-do list that did not include speaking to the person on the other end.

The easiest thing in the world to do is to ask someone at the outset of every conversation—on the phone or in person—if he or she has a moment to speak. Is this a good time? Do you have a few minutes? Am I catching you at a bad time? The concept is so simple, yet so often overlooked.

The subtext is that you respect the person with whom you're speaking and you understand that his or her time is valuable. By clearly stating who you are (introduction), why you're calling (purpose of call), and then inquiring whether he or she has the time or inclination to speak with you at that moment (key question), you establish yourself as respectful and professional. With the *key question* you generously give the other person an "out" to reschedule the call if it's not a good time or to refer you to someone else if he or she is not the right person to speak with.

Failing to start with the key question can be the difference between getting what you need (or not), making a good first impression (or not), or rubbing someone the right (or wrong) way. Are you going to achieve your intended goal if the person on the other end of the line is only half listening? Will you actually get the follow-up meeting if your counterparty has only two minutes for you and you don't think to ask if there's a better time to talk?

The Strategy: The Three-Step Hello

1. Introduction
2. Purpose of your call
3. Key question

On-the-Job Case

1. Introduction

Hi, Pam, this is Nelson Blair calling from the Juvenile Diabetes Foundation. I was referred to you by Arthur Braniff.

This is a no-brainer, but please don't assume everyone knows who you are or remembers what firm you're with (or what school you're from or how your aunt Margaret introduced the two of you last summer).

Start with your full name and, if you're affiliated with an organization, make it known up front. If you've been referred by someone else, state that clearly. Don't make the person on the other end of the line spend the first few minutes of the call racking his or her brain trying to figure out who you are or how he or she knows you.

2.   Purpose of Your Call

I am calling to follow up on the e-mail I sent you last Friday regarding next month's charity auction.

Let me know up front and center what the call or conversation is regarding. Then I can decide whether to engage, ask to speak at a different time, or suggest that you speak with someone else. Whether you have information to share, you need information, or you're reaching out on behalf of someone else, I'll be more likely to take your call if I know why you're calling or dropping by. Tell me right away so that I can shift gears to focus on the topic at hand or let you know that now is not a good time to talk.

3.   The Key Question

Do you have a few minutes to speak?

In 2009, I reached out to a business school prospect to pitch the Great on the Job training program. I had been referred to the school's director of career services, Pat Harding. After sending Pat an introductory e-mail, I followed up with a phone call. Unlike with many business-development calls I make, Pat actually picked up her own line. Here's how the conversation went:

"Hi, Pat, this is Jodi Glickman calling from Great on the Job. I was referred to you by Karin Ash at the Johnson School."

"Oh, hello, Jodi. How are you?"

"I'm great, thanks. I was wondering if you had a few minutes to follow up on the e-mail I sent you last week regarding Great on the Job and to talk about whether this might be of interest to your MBA students."

"Jodi, thanks so much for calling. Actually I'm headed into a meeting right now, but let me have Katherine Leeds follow up with you. She handles student programming."

"Okay, thanks so much, Pat. I will look forward to hearing from Katherine."

I hung up the phone slightly dejected—it was a quick call and I didn't get a chance to pitch my product. Nonetheless, I had been professional (I identified myself and stated the purpose of my call) and respectful of Pat's time (by asking her if she had a few minutes to speak, which she did not).

Pat no doubt appreciated the "easy out," given that she was headed into another meeting. The very next day Katherine Leeds gave me a call to follow up, and there began the beginning of my relationship with the business school, which I am happy to report is today a client.

Who knows what would have happened had I opened the conversation with a quick hello and launched right into the GOTJ sales pitch. Given that Pat was about to go into a meeting, she would have had to cut the conversation off early. Perhaps she would have been annoyed that

I'd interrupted her before an important meeting. She would likely have been distracted thinking about the meeting. Perhaps she would have half listened with one ear and politely said thanks, but no thanks, we're not interested, just to get rid of me.

Fortunately, I didn't have to worry about Pat's being annoyed, distracted, or eager to hang up the phone. I didn't put her in an awkward or uncomfortable position. I simply gave her an out, which she took me up on, ending the call quickly but promising to put me in touch with her colleague.

Here is some additional sample language that I could have used in my three-step hello with Pat and that you can use at the outset of any conversation.

1. INTRODUCTION

- Hi, Pat, this is Nelson Blair calling from the Juvenile Diabetes Foundation. I was referred to you by Arthur Braniff.
- Hello, this is Roger Hollis calling from the retail division at Nike.
- Hello, my name is Brendan Davies and I'm a student at the University of Michigan.
- Hi, Brent, this is Alex Harding from Vanderbilt University; Professor Thomas introduced us this spring on campus.

2. PURPOSE OF YOUR CALL

- I'm calling to follow up on the e-mail I sent you regarding next month's charity auction.
- I'd like to give you an update on the spring fund-raising campaign.
- May I fill you in on the details of last night's committee meeting?
- I'd like to ask for your help drafting a job description for the executive assistant position.

3. THE KEY QUESTION

- Do you have a few minutes?
- Is this a good time?
- Do you have a moment to speak?
- Am I catching you at a bad time?

———— • ————

The same approach works for in-person drop-bys. The three-step hello is just as critical when you pop over to your boss's or colleague's office or cubicle to give a quick update, ask a question, or just say hello. Just because the door to someone's office is open doesn't mean he's eager to stop what he's doing the moment you decide to drop by.

Will your manager drop everything she's doing and give you her full attention if you catch her at a bad time? Starting with a knock on the door followed by a "Do you have minute?" will invariably get you further in the long term than will barging into people's offices and assuming they're ready and willing to chat.

———— • ————

I'm also going to see how they treat the receptionist. I always get feedback from them. I'll want to know if someone comes in and if they weren't polite, if they didn't say "Hello" or ask them how they were. It's really important to me.

—Jana Eggers, former CEO, Spreadshirt, from *New York Times* interview "Should I Hire You? I'll Ask the Receptionist"

When my literary agent's assistant, Sara, answers the phone at Zachary Shuster Harmsworth and says, "Good morning, Zachary Shuster Harmsworth, this is Sara, how may I help you?" I immediately address Sara by name and ask her how she is doing, inquire about her weekend, or wish her a happy holiday if appropriate.

Sara and I have never met in person but we speak on the phone occasionally, and I am always gracious and considerate when we speak. If I'm rude or dismissive of Sara, disrespectful or abrupt, it's probably going to make its way back to my agent and potentially impede my access to him. After all, Sara doesn't have to pass along my message right away, track him down when I need him, or help me fax a document to him if she doesn't want to.

When an assistant answers the phone, you should add two steps to your "hello":

1. Greet by name.
2. Ask how they are doing.

Then proceed as before with your introduction, purpose of the call (whom you are calling and why), and the key question—is so-and-so available?

Here are some ideas of how to handle the opening conversation with someone's assistant.

---

1. INTRODUCTION (GREET BY NAME)

- Hi, Sara. This is Jodi Glickman calling for Todd Shuster.
- Hello, Brian, how are you? This is Patricia Palermo from Skadden Arps.
- Susan, hello, this is Erin Edwards calling from Dr. Cannon's office.
- Hello, my name is Anderson Byers and I'm a student at the University of Illinois School of Engineering.

---

2. HOW ARE YOU?

- How are you?
- How's everything going?
- Did you have a nice weekend?
- Happy New Year! Is the week getting crazy for you already?

---

3. & 4. PURPOSE OF CALL & KEY QUESTION

- I am calling to speak with Todd about the book proposal. Is he available by chance?
- I was hoping to speak with Nancy about tomorrow's presentation. Is she in?
- Is Lisa planning to be in the office this afternoon? I'd like to speak with her about the Vios account.
- I'm looking for Jordan. I need to reach him urgently before we go to press tonight.

Forward Momentum: Good-Bye

The "good-bye" is actually not an ending point, but rather a transition for your next call or conversation. With the close of every conversation, you want to leave the door open for all future interactions. A professional and courteous good-bye reinforces that you're a respectful colleague and sets the stage for positive interactions going forward.

The Strategy: The Two-Step Good-Bye

1. Thank you
2. Forward momentum

On-the-Job Case

1. Thank You

Jane, it was great speaking with you this morning, thanks so much for your help.

When someone is helpful, it's easy to end a conversation. The words *thank you so much* come to mind readily and typically give you a good way to get off the phone or leave someone's office. However, many conversations are not particularly helpful. Some are outright boring or unproductive.

Nonetheless, people deserve the courtesy of being thanked for their time, if not for their helpfulness, insight, or intuition. Even if a conversation is a total bust, go ahead and thank your counterpart for his or her time. When people take up your time, you can expect a thank-you for having shared it with them. You should do the same.

2. Forward Momentum

I will look forward to staying in touch and working together in the future.

Every conversation presents an opportunity to build upon and expand your network. With each new interaction, you have an opportunity to establish or build rapport and leverage professional relationships going forward. Building on the "thank you" is where the true skill comes in.

A hint of forward momentum—letting someone

know how or when you plan to follow up, offering to give a heads-up or a posting when things change, or just committing to share your contact details or touch base in the near term—gives you the footing you need to stay in touch and keep the door open.

Moreover, even when it looks as if there'll be no future interaction—you'll no longer be working on a project together, you didn't get the position, the other person is leaving the firm, you got what you needed, etc.—don't be fooled. You never know when you will cross paths again. Leaving one door open is infinitely easier than having to open a new one next time around.

Here is some additional sample language you can use to end your conversations skillfully and maintain forward momentum.

---

1. THANK YOU

- Jane, it was great speaking with you this morning, thanks so much for your help.
- Thank you for raising some interesting issues I hadn't considered before. You've inspired me to revisit the issue.
- Brian, thanks again for taking the time this afternoon to connect.
- Thanks for sharing your time generously. I know how busy you are.

2. FORWARD MOMENTUM

- I will look forward to staying in touch and returning the favor one day.
- I'm sorry we won't be working together, but I'd love to stay in touch and grab coffee at some point.
- I will let you know the outcome of the meeting and keep you posted on how things shake out.
- If you need any additional information from my team, please don't hesitate to ask.
- Is there anyone else you think I should speak to about lighting and set design?
- I may come back to you with further questions if that's all right?

———— • ————

Getting off to a good start is key to making good first impressions and critical to establishing long-term relationships. Using these strategies will enable you to engender goodwill with others and encourage people to take your calls or stop what they're doing to really listen to you.

Keeping the door open at the end of your conversations will allow you to create the "currency" of forward momentum, building goodwill you can use in the future for a whole host of things—asking for help or feedback, networking internally, or building external relationships to leverage throughout your career. Equally important, mastering the hello and good-bye will allow you to focus on the more important aspects of your interactions, i.e., the actual content of your message.

TROUBLESHOOTING

Q: If I drop by someone's office, should I stand or take a seat while I speak?

A: A safe rule of thumb is to stand until you are invited to sit. If you don't get an invitation to sit down, take it as a sign that this drop-by is intended to be quick—so get to your point and then take your leave politely.

Q: Sometimes I find myself trapped in a manager's office after finishing a conversation and I don't know how to exit. What should I do?

A: A great way to end an awkward (or potentially awkward) conversation is to acknowledge that people are busy and let them know that you don't want to take any more of their time.

Thanks so much, you've been very helpful. I don't want to take any more of your time.

Or, if you've been discussing an assignment or task or deal you're working on, then always appropriate is the exit-on-account-of-the-topic-at-hand option.

Okay, I'd better go finish up the memo. Or: *Thanks so much, I'm going to go ahead and call Andrea now to follow up on the report.*

Q: If I'm speaking with an important client or a senior person in my organization, should I address that person as Mr. or Ms. or use his or her first name?

A: Your default should be to address people by their first name—in person, on the phone, and via e-mail. Using first names puts you on more equal footing with colleagues and clients, even when people are senior to you.

The exception to the rule is if / when other people in your organization use more formal greetings with certain clients or executives—in that case follow their lead and do the same. If you are introduced to someone with a title, such as "This is Professor Michaels" or "I'd like you to meet Dr. Cummins" or "Please say hello to Mr. Drummond," then use that title until the other person tells you not to.

chapter two

The Foolproof Download

If I had more time, I would have written a shorter letter.

—Mark Twain

Don't bury the lead.

—Journalistic principle

While the Hello and Good-Bye are arguably the easiest communication strategies to master, one of the more difficult challenges in the workplace is the seemingly simple task of sharing information—updating your boss, posting your manager, dropping by a colleague's desk, leaving a voice mail for a vendor, or just chatting in the hallway about a project in queue. Great on the Job refers to all of these collectively as the download.

The update or download or lowdown or whatever you call it is a mainstay of any job. Unless you live like a hermit, you likely need to share information with others on a semiregular basis.

Everyone knows someone who drops by to chat and has nothing of consequence to say; everyone knows a

The Download Versus the Joke

Jokes are effective because they set up an audience with suspense before delivering a punch line at the end.

Jokes follow a rote path: setup, filler, punch line. The download is the exact opposite—it leads with the punch line.

The goal of a joke is to create suspense and maximize surprise. The goal of the download is to front-load key information and minimize surprise, confusion, or misunderstanding.

If your download sounds more like a joke (unintentionally), then this chapter is for you.

John from accounting who goes on and on in a meeting without anyone knowing what he's talking about; or Marianne in sales who gives a glowing sales report for the quarter yet leaves out the fact that you've just lost your biggest account or pulled out of the Southeast. Get to the point please.

An effective download leads with the punch line. It provides your listener with a template, or point of reference, from which to follow your synthesis of information. Rather than burying the lead, an effective download highlights the lead front and center.

The brain is not intelligent because of the sheer volume of data it can ingest, but for the way it can quickly discern patterns—and then guess the rest.

—Jeffrey M. Stibel, author of *Wired for Thought: How the Brain Is Shaping the Future of the Internet*

It is your job to analyze and synthesize information and distill the key points from a litany of facts. Knowing your data and its importance *before* you start communicating with others is the way to be an effective (and generous) communicator.

No one wants to guess at the purpose of your call or the reason behind your visit. Nothing is more irritating than a conversation that goes on and on, winds around a topic, and never gets to the point. Don't expect your listener to do the work of sorting through information to arrive at the meaning of your key points. You need to do the work for your listener.

Think of the download as an omelet. The punch line is the finished product, the dish itself. The supporting details or highlights are the key ingredients and the steps needed to make the dish. When you give someone an update, you shouldn't start by telling them about the eggs and cheese and butter or milk. Instead, you'd start off expounding the virtues of your fabulous omelet and then go into the details of what's in it and how it's made. The download is no different. Start with the big picture, the finished product, the main idea. Then narrow yourself down to talk about the ingredients and the details—the reasons why or the way in which something is happening or has happened.

You may need to share a whole host of types of updates or downloads, but this chapter will take a look at three of the most common types:

1. **The Status Update**—sharing information that is new, important, or different
2. **The Persuasive Argument**—making your case to move someone to action
3. **Missing/Outstanding Information**—sharing news in the face of imperfect information

Annika Kallo, Social Media Intern

Nancy Graeber, an entrepreneur and founder of InnoTech, a start-up Web-development firm, hated when people came into her office to give her data. "What does the data *mean*?" she would ask. Why is it important? What is new and different? Don't just tell me what the numbers *are*, tell me what they *mean*. Are expectations in line with reality? Are we ahead of our monthly targets or trailing last year's numbers? Are you happy with the trend line or do you think we're going to miss an important benchmark goal? Is there a red flag in our quarterly numbers that I need to be aware of?

Annika, InnoTech's social media intern, had recently joined the team to drive traffic to the company's Web site and enhance its Web presence across social-networking sites. Of her own accord, Annika began to post Nancy biweekly about her efforts with quick mini-briefs that Nancy greatly appreciated. Not only did Annika give Nancy the analytics and the numbers, but she also interpreted those numbers for her and shared ideas of how to capitalize on trends.

The Strategy: Status Update

1. The punch line
2. Key facts / supporting highlights
3. Forward momentum

On-the-Job Case

1. The Punch Line

*Nancy, our April numbers look great. We're at fifteen thou-
sand unique visitors for the month, which represents a twenty-
five percent increase over last month.*

The status update is intended to share information that
is new, different, or important, and the key is to let your
listener know up front and center what the bottom line,
or punch line, is. Think about your objective—what are
you hoping to get out of the conversation? Are you sharing information or do you need information? Are you
hoping to drive your boss to action or are you simply trying to keep everyone informed? Are you making a recommendation, reporting back on good news, or asking
for permission or guidance to move forward with something?

To come up with your punch line, think through what
is new, different, or important and consider answering these
questions for your listener:

- What do I need to know?
- Why do I need to know it?
- Who is doing what?
- What should I be doing?
- What is the timing?
- What other information is outstanding?

In Annika's case, her new information was that April numbers were great. If you can't answer at least two or three of the aforementioned questions, you're probably not well enough prepared. Not knowing your objective or failing to lead with the punch line will lead to a bad outcome.

2. Key Facts / Supporting Highlights

The guest blog post you did for Alistapart.com was a key force in driving that number—almost three thousand new visitors linked to us from there.

This is where the who, what, how, when, and why come into play—the salient details to support your position or update. An easy way to think about the key facts and supporting highlights is to ask yourself, What are the *reasons why* or *ways in which* something has happened? Why or how is some piece of information new, different, or important?

Again, the goal is to do the work for your boss or manager. Don't make her guess at what you want or need. If you go in to tell your manager, Alyse, that the deal is being delayed, she'll want to know why. If you go in to ask for help developing a training program for new hires, then be armed and ready with the ways in which you need help from her. If you drop by to recommend moving forward with a sales promotion, be ready to make the case for why that particular marketing tactic makes sense. Provide the key pieces of information or facts that she'll need to fully understand the situation and make a decision about moving forward. In essence, you want to be able to answer your boss's objections before she has a chance to voice them.

Another easy way to think about reasons why and ways in which is to simply use *because* to prompt your thinking. If you're making a statement, arguing your case, or sharing information, be sure you have the "because" ready and waiting as backup for the follow-up questions that will inevitably come your way. Not being able to answer the why or how is a surefire way to leave your boss or manager thinking you've done an incomplete job. Here are a few examples:

- The meeting has been canceled → because the team is stuck in Memphis.
- Our Web traffic is up thirty percent → because of last month's guest blog post for Yahoo! Shine.
- We're not moving forward with the August press release → because it was cost-prohibitive.

The Download Gut Check: Are You Using the Three C's?

- **Be concise**. *No one likes to read a one-page e-mail or listen to a four-minute voice mail if he or she doesn't have to. Be short and sweet and to the point.*
- **Be clear**. *Don't jump around topics or make people guess at your meaning or intentions. Clearly state your position, give the info you need to share, get the buy-in of your audience (if necessary), and move on.*
- **Be consistent**. *Using a consistent pattern to relay information will enable you to anticipate follow-up questions and/or think about missing pieces of information before giving someone an update—keeping you one step ahead of the curve.*

3. Forward Momentum

I'll come back to you next week with several ideas for next month's blog.

Once you've shared the important information and supporting details, then move on to the follow-up or action items. You should always be thinking two steps ahead so that your manager doesn't have to. What happens next? Who is doing what? How is the team is moving forward?

Let your manager know when he can expect to see the next draft, where the final product will be delivered, or how you're closing the loop with the engineering team. If everything is complete, then tell him you're putting the issue to bed. If there is still work to be done, what are you doing next? What do you need him to do? What does the timetable look like?

Let's go back to Nancy and Annika to see what Annika's download might have sounded like regarding monthly Web traffic.

---

1. PUNCH LINE

- Nancy, the numbers look great. We're at fifteen thousand unique visitors for the month, which represents a twenty-five percent increase over last month.
- Nancy, I want to share the good news about April Web traffic. We're up twenty-five percent to fifteen thousand unique visitors for the month.
- Nancy, I have great news about our social media efforts. Web traffic is up twenty-five percent for the month, hitting a record fifteen thousand unique visitors.
- We're on track to meet our goal of twenty thousand visitors per month by June.

---

2. KEY FACTS / SUPPORTING HIGHLIGHTS

- The guest blog post you did for Alistapart.com was a key force in driving that number—almost three thousand new visitors linked to us from there.
- Last week's blog post was the most popular by far.
- The interview you did on NPR was awesome. We received over a thousand click-throughs from our reposting of the interview on our site.
- Forty percent of new visitors came from outside the U.S.

3. FORWARD MOMENTUM

- I'll come back to you next week with several topic ideas for next month's blog.
- I'm following up on all of the comments and re-tweets the post generated.
- I'm reaching out to several people who commented and inviting them to guest-post on our site next month.
- I'm working on putting together some ideas for a monthly column.

Annika's goal was to keep Nancy abreast of new developments and make sure she was on board with Annika's efforts going forward. She made sure to give Nancy both the data and numbers and also explain the importance of those numbers (guest posting had driven a huge traffic increase). Finally, Annika finished by keeping Nancy in the loop on what the next steps were and how she was keeping the ball rolling.

Graham Atkins, Marketing Director

Graham Atkins, Nancy's marketing director, owed Nancy a recommendation regarding running an online promotion with Kupon, a Web site that offered daily deals via e-mail to consumers that had to be "tipped" or activated once enough people agreed to participate (i.e., bought the deal). The team was considering offering a start-up consulting session for $199, a highly discounted rate.

The goal of Graham's download wasn't simply to share information or provide an update. Graham had an agenda: he wanted to convince Nancy to move forward with the promotion.

Nancy was concerned about the increased traffic the promotion would drive to their site, whether or not Inno-Tech could handle the expected sudden rush of business, and if the company would actually profit from the endeavor given the deep discounts Kupon promotions typically offered.

Graham wasn't worried. He approached Nancy with an update on the team's latest thinking and gave her his recommendation. His download included the hard facts (the numbers the team expected), the supporting details (the implications of those numbers), and the next steps.

Graham's thoughtful and persuasive analysis made Nancy remember why she hired him in the first place—in a start-up environment, you need people who can think through all of the issues, present the options clearly and cogently, then make go or no-go decisions readily.

The Strategy: The Persuasive Argument

1. The punch line: Make your case
2. Key facts / supporting highlights
3. Forward momentum

On-the-Job Case

1. The Punch Line: Make Your Case

The persuasive download follows a similar structure to the status update—the punch line remains front and center. However, the punch line here is a persuasive argument aimed to make your case or drive someone to action, versus a neutral statement simply giving someone new, different, or important information.

> *Nancy, I've spent some time thinking through the Kupon offer and doing some market research, and I think we should move forward with the promotion.* **[Make Your Case]**

> *The team spent a lot of time on this and we're all in agreement—the upsides in marketing and promotion are*

significant and far outweigh the negligible impact to our P and L. **[Reason Why]**

Once you've had a chance to look at everything, let's regroup. I'd like to get a call scheduled with Kupon shortly if we do want to move forward. **[Next Steps]**

Here is some additional language Graham might have used to try to persuade Nancy to move forward with the Kupon promotion.

---

1. THE PUNCH LINE: MAKE YOUR CASE

- Nancy, we've spent a lot of time thinking through the Kupon offer and doing market research. I think we should definitely move forward with the promotion.
- Nancy, I want to follow up with you on the Kupon promotion. We've thought through all the angles and our recommendation is to move forward. Do you have a few minutes to discuss?
- I'd like to give you my argument in favor of moving forward with the Kupon promotion when you have a few minutes.
- I'm ready to make a recommendation regarding Kupon—the team is in agreement that it's a smart move.

---

2. KEY FACTS / SUPPORTING HIGHLIGHTS

- The real benefits are increased name recognition and a cost-effective marketing opportunity.
- According to our analysis, the marketing and promotional upside far outweighs the minimal economic impact.
- The upsides in marketing and promotion are significant, the profit-and-loss [P&L] impact is not.
- The impact to our P and L will be negligible, but the deal will drive revenue.

3. FORWARD MOMENTUM

- I've gone ahead and e-mailed you the scenario analysis to review at your convenience.
- Lisa and Dan are finishing up a memo detailing the impact to our staffing needs and production schedule for three possible response rates. You should have it on your desk tomorrow.
- Once you've had a chance to look at everything, let's regroup. I'd like to get a call scheduled with Kupon shortly if we do want to move forward.
- I'll put a call in to Kupon to talk about final logistics pending your sign-off.

Graham did an effective job of leading with his punch line, giving Nancy the background information behind his recommendation, and finishing with proposed next steps. He gave her the information she needed in an easily digestible format and, as a result, likely had an easier time "selling" his position than would someone who gave a disorganized, incomplete, or less-than-well-constructed argument.

———— • ————

You always make decisions based on 70 percent of the information.

—COLIN POWELL, FORMER CHAIRMAN
OF THE JOINT CHIEFS OF STAFF

People often get tripped up by the misconception that you shouldn't share information until you have all the facts. The problem is that we are almost never fully informed—we often have to act on imperfect information. If we want to have complete information, we may lose our opportunity to act in a meaningful way.

The download is no less powerful or effective when you don't have full information. You can and should still update your team or boss even in the face of missing information. The key is to acknowledge the missing information up front and have a plan for either getting the information or agreeing to move forward without it.

Heather Loesche, Environmental Advocate

Heather Loesche worked for an environmental advocacy group and owed her boss, Aaron, an update about the group's environmental impact assessment (EIA) of a wind farm in Missouri. The EIA was complete and Heather was excited to share the good news. However, before she dropped by to update Aaron, she realized she wasn't sure who was going to be managing the distribution of the report.

Heather knew that while Aaron would congratulate her on the completion of the report, he'd spend no more than two minutes on the document before immediately jumping to the next step—the distribution plan (that's why he was the boss, after all; he was always moving the ball forward). Heather's consistent use of the download structure came in handy as she thought through her message to Aaron.

The Strategy: Outstanding Information

1. The punch line: status update
2. Outstanding items
3. Forward momentum

Heather's ability to anticipate Aaron's reaction enabled her to share the good news about the completion of the report without diminishing the value of her message even in light of the unknowns about the distribution plan.

> Hi, Aaron, I just wanted to drop by to let you know that the wind farm EIA is complete. Do you have a minute to catch up? *[Punch Line]*
>
> Legal counsel has signed off and the last outstanding item is distribution—we're ready to begin thinking about getting the report into the right hands. We have initial interest from both

*the Environmental Defense Fund (EDF) and Conservation International (CI). **[Outstanding Item]***

*I am reaching out to Jack at EDF and Paige and CI this week to discuss next steps. **[Forward Momentum]***

Here are some additional ways Heather could have let Aaron know that the outstanding items were being worked out.

---

1. THE PUNCH LINE

- Hi, Aaron, I just wanted to drop by to let you know that the wind farm EIA is complete. Do you have a minute to catch up?
- Aaron, I have great news—the wind farm EIA is complete.
- Aaron, I want to update you on the environmental impact assessment for the wind farm. We've completed the report.
- I want to catch you up on the wind-farm EIA when you have a few minutes.

---

2. OUTSTANDING ITEMS

- Legal counsel has signed off on the document and we're ready to begin thinking about distribution.

- The last outstanding item is distribution—we're just now focusing on getting the report into the right hands.
- The big issue now is distribution of the report. We've initiated talks with EDF and CI to discuss.
- The next hurdle is to start thinking about distribution and whom to partner with.

3. FORWARD MOMENTUM

- I have calls in to Jack at EDF and Paige at CI to gauge interest in partnering with us.
- Bruce is working on a first draft of the distribution strategy. You should see a copy within the week.
- Once you've had a chance to review the report, we can sit down and talk about our distribution strategy.
- I'm working on setting up meetings to discuss distribution. I hope to have a rough sketch of a plan by Friday.

Because Heather used a consistent pattern, she was able to identify in advance the last outstanding item (distribution) and incorporate that topic into her download. She anticipated Aaron's concerns and was able to play offense, highlighting the issue up front, instead of playing defense—and waiting for Aaron to ask.

TROUBLESHOOTING

Q: How often should I provide my boss with a download?

A: People differ in the amount of information they need, and the frequency with which they need updates. Some managers like end-of-the-day (EOD) updates, others prefer weekly or monthly updates, and yet others only want to hear from you as needed.

   A good place to start is with a weekly update and then modify from there. If you sense your boss wants or needs more information more regularly, you can increase the frequency of that schedule; if things aren't changing that often and you have nothing new or valuable to add, then you might consider switching to an as-needed basis. See below for a sample EOD e-mail.

Q: What does a sample EOD e-mail look like?

A: Here are a couple of good examples:

Emily,

I want to let you know where things stand as of close of business today:

- The Turner report is in progress. I have finished the first three sections and expect to have a final draft to you by next Monday the latest.

- I also have several calls in to the marketing department to get their comments on our proposal. I haven't heard back from them yet, but will let you know as soon as I do.
- Allison Ravine from Starlight did respond today regarding next week's meeting—she and her team will all be there.

Please let me know if there's anything else you need from me, otherwise I will let you know if anything changes on my end.

Jodi

Stuart,

I met with Bill Lutz this morning to discuss the media team's staffing needs. He is quite anxious about his ability to get a full staff up and running within the proposed 45-day time frame. I told him I was confident in our ability to meet his needs and make it happen. Here's what we're doing on our end; there is no action required of you at this time.

- Bill needs/wants a deputy officer on board by the end of the month—we are aggressively employing our network of contacts to search for candidates to fill the position ASAP.
- Bill's team agrees that there is capacity for at least three additional reporters and researchers; we will look internally to fill those positions before doing any external outreach.

- Lastly, he needs five additional administrative posts filled. I have calls in to several staffing firms to help with this component

Again, I don't think there's anything here for you do to immediately—I will let you know if that changes. Please let me know if you have any questions in the meantime.

Austin

Q: What if I have no news to share?

A: Even when you have nothing new to share, give a quick update to state exactly that to help manage expectations and keep people from getting jittery. If your manager wants a daily update and you have nothing important to share, tell her so. Here are two examples of a no-news download:

Emily—

I just wanted to let you know there is nothing new on the Fairmont campaign proposal. I will let you know as soon as that changes.

Jodi

Stuart,

Regarding the Fairmont campaign proposal, I still have not heard back from Yvette's team. I promise to let you know the moment I hear something (I know everyone is anxious).

Best,
Austin

Q: When should I give a download in person and when is it okay to use e-mail?

A: People are always going to have preferences about how they like to receive information, so you should ask your manager or teammates what works best for them.

However, the golden rule of the download is this: contentious or controversial issues *must* be handled in person. If you're sharing bad news or having a problem with someone, you can't tell them via e-mail. Tone and tenor get lost in e-mail, and people are highly predisposed to misinterpret information delivered electronically.

If you have to ask yourself whether something will be poorly received, misconstrued, or may offend, go with a face-to-face delivery. The risk of miscommunication or argument is simply not worth it.

Q: What's the best way to deliver bad news?

A: The best way to deliver bad news is the same as good news: lead with the punch line. Don't bury the lead or try to skirt the issue. State the bad news up front and then move quickly on to the solution—how are you moving forward to remedy a problem, fix a mistake, compensate for lost business, or assuage a disgruntled customer. See Chapters 8, "Raise a Red Flag," and 9, "Manage a Crisis," for more information on handling difficult conversations.

Q: What if I have a ton of information to share? Any tips for making it easier to organize my thoughts?

A: Another important component to a successful download, especially in writing, is the use of categories. When you have lots of information to share, you absolutely must categorize the key areas or topics you plan to discuss. If you're sending an update on a project completion schedule or providing feedback on a project plan, think about the main topics you want to cover and break out your comments to fit into neat categories within the "key highlights / supporting facts" section.

Patrick Deming, a young entrepreneur, was looking to make an investment in the Handler Corporation, a magazine publisher. After several calls with the management team and a decent amount of research, Patrick decided to send Taylor, the president of Handler, an e-mail outlining his thoughts on the business and the key questions he would need answered to his satisfaction before making an investment.

Patrick's original e-mail was a two-page treatise on magazine publishing with over twenty-five questions interspersed throughout. After reviewing the e-mail, Patrick realized it presented him as scattered and disorganized. He also recognized how difficult he was making it for Handler to respond to his inquires.

After more thought, Patrick decided to group his questions into three major buckets—operational, financial, and managerial. He took another shot at revising his e-mail and was amazed at how much clearer his thinking became when he organized his thoughts and questions around three major topics.

Here's an excerpt of Patrick's e-mail to Taylor:

Taylor,

I am following up with you on our recent conversations regarding Handler. As I hope you know, I remain extremely interested in the opportunity and highly optimistic that an agreement can be reached. [Punch Line]

My enthusiasm notwithstanding, I do have a number of questions that I'd like answered as we think about moving forward. I have organized my thoughts and questions into three major categories: managerial, operational, and financial. They are as follows:

Managerial
- Has the board authorized the sale of the assets at the quoted price?
- How well do the executive publisher and editor in chief work together?
- How much time does the editor in chief spend on each title?

Operational
- How many employees do you expect to keep on full-time postsale of the company?
- Do you envision changing your publishing calendar anytime in 2011 or 2012 or do you expect to maintain all titles as monthlies?
- How many total pages to you expect per title for 2011 and 2012?

Financial
- What are net operating margins for 2009, 2010, and 2011 E?
- What percentage of the profits do you expect to pay out as a dividend?
- What percentage increase in ad sales revenue are you projecting for 2011?

Please let me know if there's anyone else I should follow up with directly regarding the questions above and/or if you'd like to schedule a call to discuss. I look forward to hearing from you at your convenience. [Forward Momentum]

Regards,
Patrick

chapter three

Be Strategically Proactive

If your ship doesn't come in, swim out to it.

—JONATHAN WINTERS, COMEDIAN

No one cares more about managing your career than you do.

—SENIOR PARTNER, WALL STREET

Alex Brahmin, Summer Intern, Keller Zabel

Getting a full-time offer at Keller Zabel was extremely competitive and required a whole lot of doing things right. Alex Brahmin was one of those poor souls who should have received a full-time offer but didn't. Being strategically proactive could have changed his fate.

Alex was a smart, inquisitive summer intern from the University of Indiana. When he first interviewed in New York City, the airline lost his luggage and he showed up in sweatpants amidst a sea of Ivy League candidates wearing dark suits. That he got the internship anyway was a testament to his potential.

Alex did a perfectly adequate job that summer. His

teams appreciated his efforts and everyone liked him. He worked on several strategic reviews for clients and received positive feedback throughout the summer. Unfortunately, when August came to a close, Alex didn't make the cut. What stood in the way of a full-time offer for Alex was that no one could actually attest to his skill set.

Alex didn't work on any challenging projects throughout the summer, whereas many of his peers got their hands dirty working on complex transactions or meaty pieces of analysis.

That Alex didn't get assigned difficult or challenging tasks wasn't entirely his fault. But it wasn't anyone else's fault either. The staffers and senior folks on his teams didn't take the time to talk to one another to find out if he was doing any heavy lifting for his other teams. On each of his teams, he did what was asked of him and did it well. But in the end, it wasn't enough.

———— • ————

Whenever you start a new job, take on a new role, or join a new organization, it's your responsibility to make yourself a useful part of the team and prove your value. The burden lies with you to make the most of your new role and to become an indispensable part of your team or organization. While others will hopefully be there to guide and lead you, it is ultimately your responsibility to get involved with meaningful and important work.

People often wrongly assume that they can't choose their own assignments or manage their own workloads. While you must take on certain tasks or assignments as part of your job description, you can manage an increasing portion of your own workflow over time.

There are always going to be plum assignments and crappy assignments. There will be tasks you enjoy and those you dislike. Moreover, some things you are good at doing and some not. The luckiest people in life are those who have found something to do that they both enjoy *and* are good at doing.

But even the most passionate and successful professionals who love their chosen profession (think the fully expressed architect or veterinarian or NFL coach) don't enjoy (and probably aren't great at) every single aspect of their job.

Being strategically proactive is this: recognizing what you're not good at doing but know to be necessary to succeed (learn); knowing what you're good at and like doing and making those opportunities happen (excel). It also includes knowing what needs to get done that no one wants to do (assist), knowing what you don't want nor need to do to succeed (redirect), and knowing whom you should work with to learn from and get ahead (network).

It's obviously not possible to do all of these things all of the time, but it is eminently possible to make some of it happen some of the time. That's your goal. If you can work on some of the things you both like and are good at, that will have a positive impact on the rest of your workload. It will give you a chance to excel in certain areas and show off your talents. If you are happier, you will do better work; if you do better work, you will continue to get better assignments. You will create a virtuous cycle for yourself that will bring about positive change in your job.

Okay, so the obvious question is: How do you make work that you like and are good at appear? How do you make work that you don't enjoy disappear? How do you work with the most well-regarded, best-connected people within your organization?

Great on the Job's LEARN strategy requires that you be extremely thoughtful and calculating when you are working with teams. If you use the LEARN strategy, you will undoubtedly contribute more, learn more, and become a more integral part of your team or organization.

The Strategy

- **L**earn
- **E**xcel
- **A**ssist
- **R**edirect
- **N**etwork

On-the-Job Case

Learn a New Skill

If you're going to be working, you may as well be learning. *Think of it as paid "research and development" into your own career.* Someone else is paying you to learn. When you stop learning, you stop challenging yourself. Your opportunities for personal and professional growth disappear. At Goldman Sachs, the modus operandi is that everyone should perform at one level above pay grade. Analysts should be doing the work of the associates; associates should act like vice presidents; and vice presidents are expected to do the work of managing directors. The moment you became complacent or comfortable with your role, you were asked to take on a new or different challenge. It was an up-or-out environment—if you weren't growing in your role, you might as well show yourself to the door.

The first and most obvious way to insert yourself proactively into any new team or group environment is to offer to work on something that you'd like to learn more about. If you are a newbie, two forces are at work. First, you typically have something of a free pass in terms of whatever deliverable or product you're assigned or offer to work on. No one expects the new guy who's still wet behind the ears to knock the ball out of the park the first time around. So take this initial grace period and try to squeeze in as much learning as you can while you still have the excuse of not being supposed to know anything, anyway.

The competing force here is fear of failure. No one wants to fail right out of the box, so the fear of failure is particularly acute when you are new. Nonetheless, being forthright about your good intentions will help your cause. Make it known that you'd like to work on the marketing brief because it will be good experience for you. Counter that by letting your team know up front you may need some help getting it across the finish line so that expectations stay in-line with reality.

In Chapter 5, "Ask for Help," you'll learn how to get the help you need on that new task, but for now, just keep in mind that you can actively manage your own learning curve and volunteer for projects and assignments that may be a stretch. These efforts will absolutely contribute to your professional development.

Excel

Good managers know that assigning people work that they are interested in and good at tends to motivate them. It's called playing to their strengths. Excelling at something you're good at is probably the easiest component of the LEARN strategy. The challenge is to make those assignments come your way.

Think about an assignment in terms of your contribution to the organization. If you know you possess a specific talent, you have good reason to proactively offer to work on a project that puts those talents to use. Your good work will benefit the organization as a whole *and* will make you look good—it's the proverbial win-win for everyone.

Assist Others

Basketball teams keep track of assists because they are critical to the success of any team. The same is true of assists in the workplace. There are two kinds of assists at work. The first is the ever unpopular and not necessarily fun administrative task. No one likes coordinating calendars with sixteen executives, counting and recounting pages of a bound presentation, or making sure copies are printed and sent by FedEx overnight. But administrative activities are important and often provide an entrée to more meaningful work. Offering to help someone with a less desirable task that needs to get done can be an effective way to get involved with a new team or a project or gain visibility with colleagues who don't already know you.

The second kind of assist is a random act of kindness. If Cara and Stacey are working late on an urgent client project and you're in no hurry to get out of the office, why not offer to edit the memo, review the presentation, or even run out and grab dinner for them before you leave?

Wouldn't you be thrilled the next time you're swamped if a colleague offered to pitch in, with no personal stake involved, just to be a team player? Wouldn't you be more inclined to help people out after they'd given you an unexpected assist on the job? Plenty of times you won't be in a position to do so, but at lots of others you can certainly pitch in and help out.

Redirect Unwanted Work

Redirecting unwanted work doesn't mean saying, "No thanks, I'd rather not," when you receive an assignment. It means accepting the task but letting your manager know that you'd like some additional opportunities going forward. For example, acknowledging that while you'd be happy to draft the briefing memo, you haven't yet attended a client meeting and you'd like an opportunity to do so in the next few months.

Redirecting unwanted work also means staying ahead of the curve—keeping your eyes and ears open and volunteering for a certain project with the hope that you'll avoid an undesirable assignment coming down the pipeline.

If you are a junior member of your team, it can be tricky to redirect unwanted work. In a moment, we'll go back to our summer intern Alex, who didn't do a good job of redirecting unwanted work and found himself without a full-time offer at the end of the summer. Alex's down-fall was that he didn't aggressively manage his workload or redirect the repetitive and nonchallenging assignments he was being given. Instead, Alex should have raised his hand for projects or deals where he could have learned the skills he needed to tackle that summer.

The example language will give you several concrete ideas of how Alex could have redirected some of his un-exciting work by offering to learn new skills, excel at what he was good at, or assist others with more meaningful work.

Network

How is it that certain people get only great assignments and have tons of visibility within an organization? Some-times it's pure luck—a project needs someone junior and Tom is available. Because Tom's done good work, his boss then recommends him for a highly coveted assignment, and the ball starts rolling. Tom gets transferred overseas and the next thing you know, he's running the London office five years later.

Tom may not remember or attribute a huge amount of value to that chance encounter with the boss years ear-lier (he'll swear it was hard work and not simply luck), but that gravy train of assignments and coincidental access to senior people did really start as a result of a simple project with the boss years earlier.

So go ahead and raise your hand and ask for opportu-nities to work with people who are senior, well-connected, or highly regarded. Someone has to help them out with key clients, major transactions, or unexciting side projects. Someone needs to write their speeches for industry conferences, carry their bags, or take notes at board meetings. Managers and executives seldom work alone. Typically, they have people helping them out, working for and with them. There's no reason that can't be you.

Your request to work on a certain project or help out a key executive or up-and-comer may be turned down, but the worst that happens is someone says no. More often than not, people react positively to proactive offers of help.

You can also make these requests indirectly. There's nothing wrong with telling your mentor you'd like an opportunity to do a rotation in the executive suite as a special assistant or telling your colleague in product development that you're itching to join his group. You'd be surprised at how fast news travels.

You can be as explicit or as cagey as you like. Ask your mentor outright what you can or should do to make that rotation happen. Or make an offhand comment about how fun it would be to see the inner workings of the executive suite. That may open up the dialogue and allow you to press the issue further about how to make the move happen.

———— • ————

Let's go back to Alex at Keller Zabel and think about how he might have used the LEARN strategy to avoid the pitfalls he encountered during his summer internship. Alex could have done several things differently to beef up his summer experience to ensure that he worked on challenging and important assignments—and, ultimately, received a full-time offer.

Learn a New Skill

Wesley, I've worked exclusively on client-service projects so far; I'd really like to do some number crunching before the summer is over. Will you please keep me in mind the next time a valuation project comes up?

Alex worked on several high-level client-service projects that summer. After the second or third project, Alex should have approached his staffer or mentor and asked for a different kind of project to round out his summer experience. It would have been entirely appropriate for him to ask for an opportunity to do some financial modeling or learn about a different financial product. He could easily have asked to work on an equity offering or see how a merger-and-acquisition transaction really worked. Would they please keep him in mind the next time a deal team or client needed an analyst for some work like that? Alex needed to lobby aggressively for his involvement in work that would be challenging and beneficial to his long-term career development.

Excel

I know you guys are putting together a sales memo. I write well and I'd be happy to review or edit a draft if you'd like another pair of eyes.

Alex was a great writer. Several summer interns helped write a sales memo for a start-up technology company. Alex could have spoken up and asked to work on that project as well or offered to review the memo—chiming in that he was a good editor. Even if he had done it on his own time and offered comments or proofreading suggestions, it would have given him a chance to show his talents.

Assist a Teammate

Ava, would it be helpful if I followed up with the Whole Foods treasurer to see when they want to schedule the next conference call?

Alex also worked on a team in the retail sector covering Whole Foods. Ava, the VP in charge of managing the Whole Foods relationship, was extremely busy and often didn't have time to give Alex much guidance. Unfortunately, Alex never offered to help alleviate Ava's workload because he wrongly assumed that she would have asked for help if she wanted it.

Had Alex been more strategic, he might have made a list of all the things going on with the Whole Foods team, gone to Ava with his list, and asked her which tasks he could help with or take off her plate. Or he could have thought ahead of time about which areas he knew he could help with and then given her a couple of options of how he might pitch in so that she didn't have to come up with work for him.

In this, the multiple-choice strategy, you give someone a choice of two or three options instead of an open canvas or blank slate. This means citing two or three specific areas in which you can help, versus simply using the open-ended

"How can I help?" We'll talk more about this later in the chapter on page 58.

Redirect Unwanted Tasks

Brian, I've done a lot of management-review pages for Luke and Peter in the last few weeks. What if I get a head start building the income model? I know you weren't going to look at that until next week, but I'd love the opportunity to get some financial-modeling practice in.

This is where Alex could have changed his fate. He got stuck doing a lot of similar, high-level work over the summer. In hindsight, on the third or fourth client engagement, Alex needed to chime in and ask to take a crack at building the income model for the client—to avoid doing the same type of management-review pages (where he listed key officers) and product breakdown pages (where he created pie charts showing the company's revenue streams) he'd been doing. Alex had done enough of these pages already, and they clearly weren't helping his cause.

Network

Susan, I'd really like an opportunity to work with Doug or Geoff in the next few weeks. Please let me know if either of their teams needs a junior analyst.

Networking in this context means creating an opportunity to work with someone new, well connected, senior in the organization, or with a reputation as a star performer.

Alex could have approached his mentor halfway through the summer and suggested that he had only worked with a handful of people and mentioned that he'd like to work with as many senior associates as possible. Perhaps he could have singled out two or three associates who were well respected and asked to be assigned to work with one of them over the next few weeks—in the hope that he'd learn from one of them or get some influential allies invested in his career development—all with the goal of landing that full-time offer.

———— • ————

Here is some additional language Alex could have used to send out an SOS to his teams that he needed some challenging or meaningful work before the end of the summer.

LEARN A NEW SKILL

- I've worked exclusively on client-service projects so far. I'd really like to do some number crunching before the summer is over.
- Will you please keep me in mind the next time a technical project comes up?
- I'd love to take a crack at the numbers on a debt deal. Will you keep me posted if anything comes up?
- I'm really hoping to build a merger model this summer. I'd be happy to start working on one for the Lauder team if you'd like.

EXCEL

- I know you are putting together a sales memo. I write well and I'd be happy to review or edit a draft if you need an extra pair of eyes.
- Jonathan mentioned his team is drafting a sales memo for the Lauder deal. Do you need another junior analyst?
- I'd love to help draft the sales memo. What if I took charge of outlining the first three sections?
- I think the Lauder deal would be a great project to get involved in. Please let me know if you need another analyst with strong writing skills.

ASSIST A TEAMMATE

- Ava, would it be helpful if I followed up with the Whole Foods treasurer to find out when they want to schedule the next conference call?
- Would it help if I put together a debt-maturity schedule? I know they recently mentioned an upcoming bond offering.
- I realize we have a lot to prepare for next week's meeting. I was thinking about putting an agenda together. Would that help you?
- I know you're sitting down with Whole Foods' management next week. Would you like me to review their quarterly financials for you before the meeting?

REDIRECT UNWANTED TASKS

- Steven, I've done a lot of management-review pages in the last few weeks. What if I get a head start building the income model?
- I know you weren't going to think about a merger model until next week, but I'd like to get some financial modeling done. What if I start on that?
- I've been reviewing my workload over the last month and I've done a lot of management review pages. I'd really like to make sure I get a chance to do some technical analysis. Could we sit down and talk about how to make that happen?
- Nick, please let me know about the next debt deal that comes in. I really want to work on one.

NETWORK

- Mark, I'd love to spend some time working with you on the Intuit deal. Please let me know if you'd like help with the engagement.
- I'd really like an opportunity to work with Doug or Geoff in the next few weeks. Please let me know if either of their teams needs a junior analyst.
- Ryan, if you need any help this week putting together your talking points for the conference, let me know. I'm happy to help out.

> • Clay, please keep me in mind as you think about adding another junior analyst to the leadership rotation. I'm very interested in the program.

Had Alex incorporated any of these strategies into his summer internship, he might have had a vastly different outcome. Given his ability to meet expectations on his individual teams, his reputation as a hard worker, and that he was well liked, it's likely that he would have risen to the occasion had he had an opportunity to challenge or stretch himself. A simple request to learn something new, assist others on a meaty piece of analysis, or redirect the umpteenth unchallenging assignment might have changed the history books.

Unfortunately for everyone, Alex lost out on the opportunity to become a full-time member of the team, and Keller Zabel lost out on hiring a high-potential candidate who simply never got the chance to prove himself.

The Multiple-Choice Strategy and Why "How Can I Help?" Isn't All That Helpful

When I'm speaking to a business school audience and I ask them how they'd insert themselves into a new team process or get involved quickly and effectively with a new team, I generally hear the same thing: "Offer to be helpful," "Ask how you can help," or "Tell them you want to be as helpful as possible and ask what they'd like you to work on."

I agree that asking "How can I help?" is better than doing nothing at all. But it's not the best you can do. On a scale of 1–10, it's about a 5. You want to be at a 10.

Elsa Kraemer was an account manager for an advertising agency whose summer intern Radja made the mistake of stopping by Elsa's office once a week to ask if she had any work for her. By the middle of the summer, Elsa had become slightly annoyed with Radja, and by the end of the summer she had written her off completely.

Elsa explained, "Had Radja ever stopped by my office to offer me help with a specific task or regarding a specific client account, I probably would have taken her up on her offer. But every week she expected me to come up with something for her to do, and I just didn't have the time to think about putting her to work."

Elsa is not alone. When someone comes to you with two specific offers of help that you can accept, deny, or modify, it's a whole lot easier than responding to an open canvas. Asking "Would you like me to put in a call to Julia or help out with the presentation outline?" is a lot easier to answer than "What can I be helpful with?" The multiple-choice strategy is exactly that: giving someone several options of how you can pitch in.

The Multiple-Choice Stategy

1. Be proactive.
2. Offer to do one or two specific things.

Benefits of Multiple-Choice Approach

- *It makes it easier for someone to take you up on an offer.*
- *You'll likely be given something else to do if your initial offer is declined.*
- *It gives you additional insight, usually a reason why your offer was declined (Laurie is already working on that, we've completed the task, we're no longer moving forward with that project, etc).*

On-the-Job Case

When you're new to an organization or working with a new team, the multiple-choice strategy can be a great way to insert yourself into the work stream.

Suppose you've just started on the marketing team at Unilever. You'll be working on the new Dove soap ad campaign. You want to show your team that you're a go-getter and you want to jump right in. What should you do?

By using a multiple-choice strategy, you'll demonstrate an initial or basic understanding of what's going on around you, and you'll make it easier on the person on the receiving end to take you up on your offer.

If your boss doesn't take you up on your offer, he'll probably give you something else to work on (mission accomplished) or explain why that task isn't necessary, which provides you with anecdotal information that gives you additional insight into your organization. For example: *Thanks, but I don't need your help on the sales report because . . . we've already finished this month's numbers; Steven is taking it over the finish line; the deadline has been pushed back; we're no longer putting that as a top priority, etc.*

Whatever the reason your offer is declined, you've just gleaned some new information to keep in your back pocket.

The more you know, the better—your new information may come in handy in another situation or just give you an idea of who's doing what, how priorities have shifted, or what your boss is currently focused on.

Following are a few concrete ways you can offer to help. You might say, *Would you like me to . . .*

(a) *gather information or*   (a) *set up a meeting or*
(b) *research sales leads?*   (b) *organize the company picnic?*

(a) *draft a memo or*   (a) *get a marketing update or*
(b) *reach out to the*   (b) *pull together a briefing*
   J & J team?   *memo?*

Here's some additional example language you can use to offer to be helpful.

---

1. BE PROACTIVE

- I'm happy to . . .
- Would you like me to . . . ?
- Why don't I start on . . .
- Does it make sense for me to . . . ?

---

2. OFFER TO DO ONE OR TWO THINGS

- Put in a call to the graphic design guys *or* put some bullet points together for the public relations launch?
- Work on a first set of slides *or* put in a call to Eileen to close the loop on the outstanding contract issues?
- Reach out to Chris to set up a call *or* pull the materials together for you to review?
- Circle back with Rob and Nicole to see where the group stands *or* start reviewing the strategic plan?

TROUBLESHOOTING

Q: How can I be strategically proactive when I've got an extremely demanding workload with no room to breathe?

A: Keep track of what you're working on and identify the areas where you are either (1) excelling or becoming an expert or (2) not getting any exposure or experience. The goal is to balance out the two and move on from areas where you've become expert and make sure to gain experience in the areas where you're lacking exposure.

Excelling or Becoming an Expert

When you feel you've maxed out on the learning curve, it's time to raise your hand and ask for additional responsibilities or new projects. Going back to the *L* in our LEARN strategy, you always want to be learning and growing in any role. Once that learning curve flatlines, you've got to think about ways to steepen it again and stretch yourself to new assignments.

No matter how busy you are, if you're not growing and contributing to the firm, you're bound to become dejected or de-energized—neither of which is good for you or your firm. If that happens, you have a responsibility to let your manager know that you need to think about shifting a portion of your workload to areas that are new and different and challenging to you, allowing for your personal growth and opening up opportunities for junior people to get experience tackling the areas you've now mastered.

Here is some example language you can use:

- Liz, I'm basically doing market research reports in my sleep these days. I'd really like an opportunity to challenge myself and get some client interaction under my belt in the next few months.
- Sean, I've spent the last year really honing my market research skills and I'd like to give some junior folks an opportunity to get involved. I'd also love some opportunities to expand my own skill set. Can we talk about some ways to make that happen?

Not Getting Any Exposure or Experience

Equally important, when you identify areas that are lacking in your skill set, it's important to address them head-on and come up with ways to fill in the gaps. There is no personal road map that gets you from point A to point B in any career, but people who move up the ranks tend to know their areas of weakness and compensate for them or make sure to address them head-on by learning new skills.

You don't want to be the kind of professional who has "one year's experience, repeated twenty times." Asking for work in areas that you identify as gaps in your skill set will benefit both your professional development and your ability to contribute to your organization.

Here is some example language you can use:

- Maria, I haven't written a marketing brief yet and I've been with the company for over a year. I'd like to make sure to get that experience soon.
- Justin, I've been thinking lately about my lack of client interaction. I haven't had the same level of opportunity that I had hoped to have by this point. I'd like to talk about ways to fix that.
- I want to discuss taking on some new assignments in the next few months. I really want to run a client focus group and hand over some of the market research stuff I've been doing to Allison.

Q: What if I've used the LEARN strategy and I'm still not getting good assignments?

A: In this scenario you should talk to your manager about why your efforts to strengthen your skill set are not being well received. You need to understand your manager's goals as they relate to your own career development, then figure out how or why your ideas of career advancement are not in line with your manager's ideas.

If your supervisor says, "I don't want you working on this new project or working with another division," you need to understand why and figure out an alternative strategy to get good assignments that works in tandem with her goals for you.

Here is some example language you might use in a conversation about how you can improve the quality of your workload:

- I'm trying to actively expand my skill set and I get the sense that you're not on board with that. Is there a reason this isn't working for you?
- Megan, do you have an issue with me working with the marketing team on this?
- I'd like to schedule a conversation to discuss my workload over the next six months. I want to make sure I get some client interaction under my belt or, if that's not going to be possible, understand why not.
- Jason, I feel like we're not on the same page regarding my career opportunities here. Could we sit down to talk about your expectations of me?

Q. Will people think I'm a brownnoser if I'm trying to use the LEARN strategy?

A: The goal is to demonstrate that you're thinking about both your own career development and your contribution to the team. When utilized properly, it shouldn't sound like brownnosing. If you take on additional responsibilities or opportunities, you're likely to open up new opportunities for those junior to you. If you can work with a cross-divisional team you've long admired, then you're bound to bring that learning and experience back to your team. Or, by nurturing relationships that help you do your own job better or faster or easier next time around, you're better positioned to make others look good as well—by bringing them under your wing or having more time to contribute to their projects. If you keep both objectives in mind, you should have an easier time using the LEARN strategy.

part two

move up the learning curve

chapter four

Manage Expectations

Formula for success: under promise and over deliver.

—Tom Peters, author of
In Search of Excellence

To raise someone's expectations and then not meet them is worse than mediocrity.

—Seth Godin, author and blogger

Is there anything worse than not living up to expectations? Since the beginning of time, parents have cautioned children against getting their hopes up—expecting too much is a surefire way to end up disappointed. From something as simple as going to see the talked-about movie of the year, to saving up for a weekend away, people respond amazingly differently depending on their preconceived notions of an experience. The low-budget indie film that takes America by storm has a much smaller hurdle to clear winning over audiences than the studio-produced must-see that limps along nicely only to be declared a flop for failing to meet its outsize expectations.

The same holds true for you at work. The worst thing you can do is underperform or fail to meet someone's expectations. Handing in a report late never looks good. Going over budget on a project—not what a client wants to hear. Failing to meet your boss's requirements on a key task—an absolute recipe for disaster.

In the same way Coke's share price takes a beating when the company misses earnings, you'll take a hit professionally when you agree to do something that you can't, in the end, actually do. Isn't it amazing that Coke might earn $2.00 per share at year end, a 20 percent increase over the previous year, yet if that number was projected at $2.01, the company will get hammered by analysts and shareholders alike for failing to meet expectations?

We're all in the business of making our best educated guess—on when we can complete a report, what a project will cost, or how a finished product will look. The best we can do is set realistic expectations from the get-go, then do our best to manage and adjust those expectations as we move forward.

Connor Hodges, Junior Staffer, State Government

Connor Hodges was a junior staffer for his state legislature. Prior to his current role, he spent two years working for his local congresswoman, a hands-on manager who involved herself in the nitty-gritty details of Connor's work. Connor's new boss, Carolyn, was quite the opposite. He had a ton of work on his plate but not a whole lot of guidance. To complicate matters, he frequently fielded requests from Dan, the chief of staff, and Adam, the deputy legislative director. Connor confided to friends that he was exasperated trying to figure out what to do first and for whom he really worked.

Connor wasn't alone in being a new and relatively junior staffer balancing multiple projects, juggling numerous tasks, and trying to stay as focused as possible. He also wasn't alone in wondering whose request was more urgent—Carolyn's, the chief of staff's, or the legislative director's? After all, only Carolyn was technically his boss, but all three were senior to him. How was he supposed to effectively prioritize and manage expectations in this free-for-all environment?

After his first few months of reporting to multiple people and feeling overwhelmed by competing assignments, Connor realized he needed to make a change. He had suffered too many near misses working all night only to come in the next morning way behind on everything else piled up on his desk. Connor knew this strategy of saying yes to everyone and everything could only last so long before it eventually blew up in his face. Sooner or later he was bound to disappoint.

Connor decided to try a new tack. He resolved to take more control of his schedule and learn to speak up about setting realistic timing and goals for his projects. He still wanted to be seen as the can-do guy, but he realized simply saying yes wasn't the answer.

———— • ————

It's almost impossible to avoid falling short of expectations when you're continually in over your head, pushing the limits of available time or know-how to get things done and done well. Too often, young employees worry that they'll look inept or irresponsible in the eyes of their supervisor if they voice concern about a project's timeline or goals. Nonetheless, accepting a task you are ill suited for or simply don't have the time or resources to complete will invariably come back to bite you in the behind.

To succeed, you've got to manage expectations. You must clearly communicate your timing, status, and priorities to ensure that everyone is on the same page. When you don't know how to do something, be sure to ask for the help you need (see Chapter 5, "Ask for Help"). If you're going to need additional resources, be sure to ask for those too.

If you have the resources but not the time, you need to give your manager a heads-up and propose some possible solutions. You should acknowledge that you're willing to work hard as a matter of course, but your manager needs to know about the competing demands on your time. Once that's out in the open, you can work together to come up with a timetable or division of labor that makes sense for everyone. Transparency will go much further than false promises and late or shoddy deliverables.

The Strategy: Prioritize

1. Know your to-do list.
2. Communicate your action plan.
3. Ask for confirmation/feedback.

On-the-Job Case

1. Know Your To-Do List

Your first step in managing expectations is simply to think through and prioritize your workload. This is being proactive at its most basic. You should always have a personal road map of what is on your plate at any given moment. Whether you keep a daily, weekly, or monthly to-do list, or you have separate agendas and checklists for different teams or projects, you must always know what you need to do by when.

If you can't come up with your own work plan of how to get things done, you'll never be able to effectively manage others' expectations of you. How can you commit the appropriate time or energy to competing teams, projects, or deadlines if you don't know how much time and energy you actually have to put to work?

So keep a running list and figure out a system that works for you. I've had a document entitled "Glickman Running To-Do" for about ten years now. I never make it through my list entirely, but I always know everything that is on my plate, and I can quickly gauge my level of busyness for a day, week, or month at a moment's notice.

This to-do list is for you. The step that follows is for your boss.

2. Communicate Your Action Plan

Here's how I've been thinking about timing on the T-Mobile account: I'm going to take care of X, Y, and Z by the end of

next week and then move on to A, B, and C as soon as I
finish up.

Once you know what the next day, week, or month looks like for you, then you need to share your proposed course of action with your manager to get buy-in and make sure she's on the same page. The goal is to avoid spending 80 percent of your time invoicing customers when your manager, Susan, thinks you're spending only 20 percent of your time on that. Or, if she assumes you're spending 50 percent of your time drafting press releases and you've not started a single one, you're going to have a problem.

The idea is not to give your manager a rundown of how you spend every minute at work. The goal is to give her the broad brushstrokes of what is on your plate, what your timing looks like for key tasks, and when you expect to deliver on key assignments or have the capacity to move on to new projects.

Communicating your action plan shows that you're in control. Instead of asking your manager for outright direction on what to do and when to do it, set your own agenda. You make the decisions and effectively give your boss veto power—if something doesn't look or sound right, you can change course. But if you're moving in the right direction, you can just continue on your merry way and keep your boss posted on your progress. The hope is that most of the time, you'll be moving in the right direction.

3. Ask for Confirmation/Feedback

How does that sound to you? Does that timing work?

Once you've laid out your plan of action, make sure your manager is in agreement. The goal is to align your objectives with those of your boss, make sure she knows the direction you're moving in, and get her sign-off on the amount of time and energy you're devoting to specific tasks. Getting on the same page up front is always easier than reversing course later on.

Moreover, asking for confirmation or feedback (as opposed to asking for outright direction on timing, prioritizing, etc.) elevates your status and puts you on a more equal footing with your boss. Proposing a plan of action and then confirming that "we're on the same page" puts you in a position of strength and shows that you've got good judgment and some degree of authority to control your own fate.

Here is some example language of how a conversation around prioritizing and managing expectations might sound.

2. COMMUNICATE YOUR ACTION PLAN

- Here's how I've been thinking about timing on the T-Mobile account. I'm going to take care of X, Y, and Z by the end of next week and then move on to A, B, and C as soon as I finish up.
- I'm finishing up the report this morning and will turn my attention to your cover letter this afternoon. I expect to have both done by tomorrow.
- I'm going to draft the project scope this week. I will have a timetable and a proposal by the end of next week, and I'll be ready to present to the board by the end of the month.

- I'm planning to incorporate Michael's comments into the presentation tonight and get them to you first thing tomorrow morning. I will then be ready to get legal counsel to sign off on the document next week.

3. ASK FOR CONFIRMATION/ FEEDBACK

- How does that timing fit in with your agenda?
- Are we on the same page?
- Does that seem like the right approach?
- Would you rather I start updating the database first or continue to draft the memo for Jonathan?

Laying out your plan and getting confirmation puts you on more equal footing with your boss and shows that you've taken initiative to figure out how to get things done. Using this strategy will help you put yourself in the driver's seat and better manage your workload and expectations.

————— • —————

Being proactive won't always be enough, however. At times you've got to go one step further and actually manage expectations in response to a deluge of incoming requests or assignments.

After several months on the job, Connor realized he was drowning in too much work. All the prioritizing in the world flew out the window when he was constantly being bombarded with incoming tasks from all different directions. To manage his workload effectively, Connor was going to need to do a better job responding to inbound requests. If effect, he needed to begin playing defense.

Connor had made the mistake of assuming that every time someone asked something of him, it was urgent. He never bothered to ask anyone's timing because he assumed if people asked him to do something, they wanted it done ASAP. A colleague finally explained to Connor that this usually was not the case, which helped him to reevaluate how he approached his work.

Connor was so afraid of looking bad, of not being a team player, of showing even a hint of questioning regarding timing and expectations, that he preferred to simply accept whatever task was asked of him and then figure out how and when to do it. Invariably, this strategy left him scrambling furiously, forever trying to catch up with his to-do list and never quite certain of whether he was meeting expectations.

The Strategy: Manage Expectations

1. Ask for timing/expectations.
2. Be transparent about your workload.
3. Propose action plan.

On-the-Job Case

1. Ask for Timing/Expectations

I'd be happy to start doing some research on housing starts in the county. What does your timing look like? How urgent is this?

The more background information you have about a given task, the more likely you are to be successful. You should always ask for people's timing up front on a project if they don't offer up any details. It shows that you're actively trying to manage your workload and meet expectations.

Once you understand your manager's expectations, you can then respond that you'd like some time (an hour, or a day or two, depending on the assignment) to think about whether the timing and parameters are feasible. Then go back and confirm with your manager that this works. If the expectations are unrealistic or overly aggressive, move on to step 2.

2. Be Transparent About Your Workload

I'm happy to write the report, but I have three industry reviews due for Sara on Friday. I realistically won't have any flexibility until Monday, unless it's urgent, in which case I can get started on it this weekend.

If someone's timing or project parameters aren't doable, let the person know what else is on your plate and propose a timeline that works for you. You'll do better stating up front a realistic goal rather than agreeing to an unrealistic deadline you have no chance of meeting.

Again, the goal is to make sure you and your manager are on the same page. Being transparent and proactive are the best defenses you have. Communicating your workload to your manager shows that you're not trying to avoid a deadline because you've got concert tickets or you're rushing home to watch the NBA finals. Presumably, you're raising the issue of a deadline because of the other important projects on your plate and the fact that you don't want any of them to suffer. (If it *is* concert tickets or a hoops game you're skipping out for, you're less likely to win your case.)

3.   Propose Your Revised Timing / Action Plan

Wednesday is probably realistic to get something to you based on everything else I've got on my plate.

Once you've had time to think about the assignment, then go back to your manager with a proposed timeline and action plan in hand. Let her know that next Wednesday will work to complete the climate-change report; or, it's going to be tough to finish up the commerce and labor study by March 1 without help from a research assistant or some relief on the finance and appropriations bill you're reviewing for the chief of staff.

The goal is to devise a plan that works for both you and your boss. Once you understand your timing and ability to deliver on what's being asked of you, you'll be better able to coordinate with your boss so that both of your needs can be met—she can receive her report on a reasonable date and you can get the work done well and within the scope of work required.

Let's take a look at what Connor's conversation with Carolyn might have sounded like in response to her latest request as he tried to manage her expectations.

1. ASK FOR TIMING/EXPECTATIONS

- I'd be happy to start doing some research on housing starts in the county. What does your timing look like?
- Carolyn, do you know when you'll need the economic development report by? Do you want it to look similar to the report the team put together last year?
- What is your turnaround time on the utility legislation? Do you have any flexibility, or do you think the committee's June 1 deadline is a hard stop?
- I'd love some guidance from you on the key three sections and how you want them structured.

2. BE TRANSPARENT ABOUT YOUR WORKLOAD

- I'm happy to write the report; however, I've got three industry reviews due for Sara on Friday.
- I'm tied up with Eduardo on the education committee notes until Monday. I can start on it Tuesday.
- I imagine it should take no more than twenty-four hours to give you what you need, but let me confirm with you later this afternoon.
- I'm putting the finishing touches on the jobs report, and I've got to get Diana an update by Wednesday.

3. PROPOSE ACTION PLAN

- I'd like to think about timing and come back to you at the end of the day with a realistic timeline.
- I'll review the materials and call you by the end of the week with my timing.
- Based on everything I've got on my plate, Tuesday is a good target date to get you something.
- Leah, I'm good to go for this Friday. I'll have what you need by the end of the day.

Communicating your timing allows you to manage your workload, set reasonable deadlines, and allocate adequate time for individual tasks. Being transparent also ensures that others are aware of, and on board with, your approach.

Pushing Back

What happens when you're asked to do something (or simply directed, forget the "ask") that you can't possibly do—you simply don't have the capacity. How do you respond?

Just as blindly accepting a task that you don't know how to do is never a good idea (see Chapter 5, "Ask for Help"), neither is accepting an assignment that you don't have time for. If you're maxed out, it's imperative to communicate up front to your manager that you can't meet a specific deadline. Hiding the truth typically gets you in far more trouble than raising a red flag early and coming up with an alternative solution to stay on point, on task, and on time.

Deborah Lopez, Junior Editor, Happyprints.com

Deborah Lopez was a junior editor with the layout and design team at Happy Prints, an online printer of modern photo cards, invitations, and announcements. Deborah reported to two senior editors, Michael and Sarah, who oversaw a team of editors and production specialists.

Business was highly cyclical at Happy Prints, with lead times for custom orders often doubling during the busy holiday season. Deborah had been a newly minted junior editor in November when orders started rolling in faster than the Happy Prints team could handle. Suddenly, Deborah was responding to requests not only from Michael and Sarah, but from other team leaders in different divisions, and from other more senior editors.

Deborah was exasperated. She was putting in long days and quickly realized that she couldn't possibly meet everyone's competing requests and deadlines. Deborah realized she was going to have to manage her workload aggressively to keep her head above water with her bosses.

In this case, managing expectations wasn't enough—Deborah needed to go one step further and push back on her team to avoid an impossible situation. Deborah needed to propose an alternate solution instead of just communicating her plan of action to her colleagues and supervisors at Happy Prints.

When the next person came knocking with a request or demand or plea for help, Deborah was armed and ready to respond.

The Strategy: Push Back

1. Highlight issue/problem.
2. State rationale.
3. Propose a solution.

Jason, I'd love to help you out with your project, but I'm totally swamped right now. **[Highlight Issue]**

I'm on deadline for four invitations over the next forty-eight hours. Unfortunately, I have no time to review your edits. **[State Rationale]**

I can do one of two things for you. I can take a look at your projects starting Thursday, or I can reach out to Michael to see if he can find someone else to review these invitations for me so I can take a look at your work earlier. **[Propose a Solution]**

Here is some additional example language Deborah could have used when she was being asked to do more than was humanly possible.

1. HIGHLIGHT ISSUE/PROBLEM

- Jason, I'd love to help you out with your project, but I'm totally swamped right now.
- Mark, I do want to help, but we're under tight deadlines this week, as you can imagine.
- Elizabeth, you know I always do the best I can for you, but I'm working at one hundred percent capacity this week and won't have any flexibility until next week.
- As much as I'd like to say yes, there's really no way I can pitch in today.

2. STATE RATIONALE

- I'm on deadline for four invitations over the next forty-eight hours. Unfortunately, I have no time to review your edits.
- I have six invitations to sign off on before Wednesday. I won't be able to look at yours until Thursday, the earliest.
- The holiday orders are rolling in; there's no possible way I can take a look at your proofs this evening.
- I've got a backlog several days deep. I can't agree to anything else until I've cleared my deck.

3. PROPOSE A SOLUTION

- I can do one of two things for you: I can take a look at your projects on Thursday, or I can reach out to Michael to see if he can find someone else to cover for me so I can take a look at your work earlier.
- The best I can do is offer to help next week or see if anyone on my team has any ability to help you out tonight.
- If you want to ask Sarah to push out any of my current deadlines, feel free to do so and I'll help you out if she gives the go-ahead.
- Why don't I do my best to finish up these invitations in the next twenty-four hours and then clear my deck so I can help you out next week?

With this strategy, Deborah was respectful but firm. She was transparent in stating her rationale for not being able to help out, and she was generous and showed initiative by offering to come up with an alternative solution when she wasn't able to pitch in or help out immediately.

By using the strategies outlined in this chapter, you will communicate to others that you're in control, you're on top of the situation, and you're not going to let anything fall through the cracks—all of which will be hugely beneficial to positioning yourself as a star performer.

TROUBLESHOOTING

Q: What if my boss is a micromanager and wants to know what I'm doing all the time?

A: While managing expectations is important in all contexts, it's particularly helpful for working with difficult bosses who micromanage. Reaching out and communicating your workload or action plan regularly can eliminate the need for your boss to continuously ask you what you're working on, where things stand, or why something hasn't yet reached his desk. In theory, you'll answer his questions/objections ahead of time and potentially give yourself some space to breathe.

Daily or weekly updates or status reports are a good way to go. The frequency and level of detail will depend on what your manager expects of you. Some people like receiving a brief end of day (EOD) e-mail that gives them an update on where things stand. Other managers like a weekly report. Some employees find it easier to update or post their manager every few days as needed—when they have new or different information.

Keep in mind that an EOD or weekly e-mail should follow the rules of the Foolproof Download in Chapter 2 (page 19). The goal is clarity and brevity—start with the punch line and only include what is new or different—or acknowledge the status quo with a quick line that says "no update" so that your boss knows the last update you sent is still the most recent.

A couple of sample EOD e-mails appear at the end of Chapter 2, "The Foolproof Download," on pages 36 to 38.

Q: What should I do about the million and one requests my boss sends me? She's constantly calling and e-mailing to ask where something is before I've even had a moment to look at it.

A: When people don't hear back from you to acknowledge receipt of their request, they get nervous. Just because you know you're working on something—you've got a call in to the marketing department or you're waiting to hear back from a vendor—doesn't mean your boss knows this. Even when you're totally on top of things, there's no way for your manager to know unless you tell her explicitly and keep her in the loop.

The professional (and generous) thing to do is to *always* respond to e-mail or voice-mail requests in a timely fashion. ("Timely" depends on your organization and your relationship with your colleagues and managers, but a twenty-four-hour turnaround time is a good point of reference; adjust upward or downward from there depending on the urgency of the request and the culture of your organization.)

Sending a quick note to confirm receipt of a request or give a quick status report typically removes much of the "What's going on?" anxiety from your boss. This means **"closing the loop"** or acknowledging an inbound request upon receipt. To close the loop, do one or both of the following:

1. Confirm receipt of request/assignment/task/e-mail, etc.
2. Give your manager an idea of your proposed timing or promise to keep her in the loop as you figure it out.

Here is some example language of what your closing-the-loop e-mail might look like:

- Rachel, just received your e-mail. I put a call in to Howard this morning. I will let you know when I hear back from him.
- A.J., I received your request. I'm starting to get the ball rolling and I will let you know as soon as I have an update or better sense of timing for you.
- Leslie, thanks for your note. I am traveling but will respond tomorrow in detail—in the meantime, I've put this on my radar for first thing next week.
- Halee and David, apologies for the delay in response. I've been tied up all morning in a donor meeting. Let me take a day to think about the right approach on this and I will come back to you both with a plan of action shortly.

Q: What if I don't know how long an assignment will take to complete? How do I propose a realistic timeline?

A: When you don't know how long something will take, ask to get back to your boss or manager after a reasonable period (an hour, an afternoon, a couple of days at most) with a better estimate of when you can complete the task. Then do some homework—reach out to colleagues, ask your friends if they've done something similar, do some research online. Once you've done your homework, you can go back to your manager with a reasonable time frame and/or to get the additional guidance you'll need.

Alternatively, let your manager know that you'll need to get started on the task before committing to a final deadline. Once you've gotten started, you should be better able to gauge how long the rest of the project will take. You can then go back to your manger with a better sense of timing or a proposed date of completion.

Here is some example language you can use to ask for additional time:

- Carrie, I received your request. I'm starting to get the ball rolling and I will let you know when to expect the report as soon as I have a better sense of timing.
- Melissa, let me take a day or two to think about the right approach on this and I will come back to you with a plan of action shortly.
- Daphne, thanks for your request. I'm not sure how long it will take to reach out to key stakeholders, but I will make several initial calls and come back to you with a better gauge on timing later this week.

A helpful tip is to put a calendar alert in your Outlook or Google calendar to remind you to go back to your boss in a day or two with your timing.

Q: What happens when my manager repeatedly dumps work on me at the last minute and expects me to drop everything for his latest *urgent* request?

A: In a one-off situation, urgent requests come in and we all must respond to them. If the pattern persists, however, you've got to find a way to make it stop. The goal is to gradually train your boss to understand the consequences of last-minute, high-priority, and urgent requests. There are only so many hours in a day. Even if you are willing or able to work 24-7, dropping what you're doing now to work on something else inevitably impacts the rest of your workload.

Something has got to give. You'll either have to delay finishing up the guest list you're compiling, cancel the meeting you have scheduled for this afternoon, or let Samantha know that her seating chart you were planning to complete this evening won't be ready until tomorrow.

As always, transparency is key. To figure out what you or your boss can do differently to avoid these situations going forward, consider the following.

The Strategy

1. Highlight the issue.
2. Ask for rationale/reason.
3. Propose a solution.

1. HIGHLIGHT THE ISSUE

- Jared, do you have some time to talk about the Turner deal? I think we should discuss how to avoid another last-minute urgent project if we can.
- I'm always happy to help out, especially when last-minute things come up urgently. However, it's happening a lot and it's impacting my ability to complete my other work.
- I'd like to talk to you about coming up with some options to avoid all of these last-minute requests.
- I'd like to talk to you about the seemingly endless urgent requests that are coming in from the strategy team.

2. ASK FOR RATIONALE

- Is there a reason in your mind we seem to always be responding to urgent, last-minute requests from the client?
- Why do you think we keep getting caught with these last-minute requests from the R and D team?
- Is there anything I can do to better prepare for these situations?
- Do you see more of these requests coming in, and if so, do you have any ideas of how to make the process less painful?

---

3. PROPOSE A SOLUTION

- Are there ever any situations where an assignment comes up before you tell me about it—i.e., do you know before you tell me?
- Can you communicate it to me earlier so that I have more advance notice and I can plan ahead accordingly?
- Would it be helpful if I gave you a weekly update of what's on my plate so that you know what I'm working on?
- Is this just the nature of the business? If so, do I need to lighten my workload on some other front so that I can keep some excess capacity for these requests?

Q: What if my boss and I are not seeing eye to eye on timing and expectations?

A: If you and your boss have totally different views on how long something will take (she thinks it's easy and you know it's going to take all night), then be bold and have a discussion about alternative steps that can be taken. Here are some sample questions you can ask to convey your message.

- Can I bring in someone else to help out? I think this is going to take a while.

- Is there anything I can put on the back burner in the meantime and then revisit once this high-priority project is finished?
- Is there any way we can adjust the timetable slightly to make it more manageable? I think this is going to be a ton of work for one person.
- Would it be okay if I come in later on Thursday, as I know this is going to be an all-nighter?

Whatever the situation, it's always better to have the conversation up front. Agree on a plan of action so that you and your boss are on the same page— you both have access to the same information, you both understand the challenges associated with a particular assignment, and you're both aware of the time, energy, and resources needed to take this particular task across the finish line.

chapter five

Ask for Help

People who are successful are the ones who ask for help. It sounds simple, but to get an organization to believe that asking for help is a sign of strength, and not weakness, is huge.

—WILLIAM D. GREEN, CEO OF ACCENTURE

It is better to know some of the questions than all of the answers.

—JAMES THURBER, HUMORIST,
ALGONQUIN ROUND TABLE MEMBER

There is no such thing as a stupid question, only stupid answers.

—CONVENTIONAL WISDOM

Do you know how to do 100 percent of what will be asked of you over the next three, six, or twelve months? How much of what you need to know do you actually know? How much do you think other people know? Could it possibly be that everyone knows more than you? Sometimes it feels that way.

Robert E. Kelley, author of *How to Be a Star at Work*

and a professor at Carnegie Mellon's Graduate School of Industrial Administration, studied what he termed the *knowledge deficit**, or the percentage of knowledge people need to do their jobs well that is actually stored in their mind. His findings were amazing—the percentage ranged from as high as 75 percent to as low as 10 percent.

Ten percent—think about that for a moment. In today's knowledge-based economy, that means there's a significant knowledge deficit in every single brain-powered job. So assuming you answered no to the 100 percent question, take comfort in that you are not alone. Nobody knows everything. The challenge for all of us is to minimize that deficit by being continuously in learning mode and by asking for and getting the help we need regularly.

———— • ————

Senior managers know that asking for help is a good thing—it demonstrates good judgment and initiative. But that philosophy often differs in theory and in practice. Employees with less experience or credibility often have difficulty putting this principle into practice.

The most obvious (and frequent) reason people don't ask for help is because they are afraid of looking stupid. They fear showing their hand and admitting they don't know how to do something. Or they assume they're supposed to know an answer and decide to figure it out on their own. While being resourceful in figuring things out

* Robert E. Kelley, *How to Be a Star at Work: 9 Breakthrough Strategies You Need to Succeed* (New York: Times Business/Random House, 1998).

is by all means admirable, there's nothing worse than sitting at your desk at 9:00 p.m. spinning your wheels and struggling alone on an assignment you don't know how to do.

The goal of this chapter is to help you avoid that scenario.

Isabel Adams, Property Manager, Affordable Housing

Isabel Adams was hired as the director of property management for a small nonprofit in New York City looking to expand into development and management of affordable housing. Isabel knew the property management business cold—she had spent five years overseeing a portfolio of five hundred units of multifamily housing at her previous job.

Isabel's mandate was to build out a property management business for her new organization. She had been hired because of her proven operational experience and her no-nonsense style of dealing with landlords and tenants. One of the first thing Isabel's boss, Steven, asked her to do was to put together a business plan for the budding property management group. Isabel obliged. Four weeks later, she turned in a document that was not at all what Steven had envisioned. Upon initial review of the document, Steven realized three things:

1. Isabel had never written a business plan.
2. Isabel didn't know what a business plan looked like.

Tips for Asking for Help

• *Don't pepper people with nickel-and-dime questions. Instead, ask for a full dollar, i.e., get all of your questions answered at once instead of coming back to someone several times in the same day or week.*
• *Be smart about whom you ask. Spread your requests around— don't always ask the same people for help.*

3. Steven would have to write it himself or find someone else to do it.

Failed business plan notwithstanding, Isabel was a strong performer who had come highly recommended to her new organization. That she had never written a business plan before didn't mean she wasn't smart or capable, it just meant she didn't have the expertise or experience for that particular task.

Unfortunately for Isabel, she didn't ask for the help she needed up front. What ensued was a complete waste of time, resources, and energy on the parts of both Isabel and Steven. Isabel spent four weeks spinning her wheels, struggling on a task she wasn't equipped to do, while Steven moved along under the impression that he'd have a deliverable in hand at the end of the month. Both were sorely disappointed with the outcome when Steven told Isabel that her business plan was essentially useless.

Just because Isabel was good at *running* a property management business (i.e., collecting rents, communicating with landlords and tenants, enforcing compliance and safety) didn't mean that she'd be good at *writing* a business plan about building a property management business.

Let's take a look at what Isabel could have done differently to ensure a better outcome.

The Strategy: The Smart Ask

1. Be proactive.
2. Ask for resources/guidance.
3. Request feedback or offer milestones.

On-the-Job Case

1. Be Proactive

Steven, I'd be happy to start working on a business plan. However, I've never actually written one before.

A good attitude goes a long way when you're in the face of an "I don't know how to do something but I'm willing to learn." For Isabel, it was totally appropriate for her to acknowledge that she had never written a business plan, while still stating her willingness to take on the task.

2. Ask for Resources/Guidance

Do you have any recommendations of people I can speak with who may be able to help?

Take advantage of the collective expertise around you and ask for the resources you think will help—a recent example, someone who's worked on a similar project, an outline or a template, etc. You'll be amazed at what's available to you if you simply ask the right questions.

These types of resources are known as low-hanging

fruit—there's nothing easier than asking for an example of a similar type of work product. Don't reinvent the wheel. Instead, find out if something similar already exists. Nine times out of ten someone who works with you, close to you, or for you has worked on something similar. If Javier in marketing wrote a business plan last year for the marketing group, why not ask for a copy? If Allison in product development has source code that works, why would you ever start over from scratch?

3. Request Feedback or Offer Milestones

I'd like to put together a list of bullet points for you to take a look at to make sure we're both on the same page before starting on a full draft.

Unfortunately, many of us aren't lucky enough to receive a good example or have access to the perfect person to guide us along the way. If you don't have a neat and pretty template or document waiting there for you to follow, you've got to come up with a plan B.

In this case, plan B entails offering to come up with interim steps or milestones along the way for getting feedback from your manager. Interim steps might include an outline or rough sketch of project parameters, bullet points on the key sections to cover in a memo, or an overview of a timetable and responsibility list for an implementation plan.

In Isabel's case, interim steps could have included an outline of the business plan for Steven to review, a draft of a single section first, or bullet points on the three key points for each section.

At the very least, using this strategy would have enabled Isabel to involve Steven in the process *while* she was working, rather than waiting until the very end to confirm he was on board with her approach—which, as it turns out, he wasn't. Getting the buy-in of your manager early on to confirm what direction to follow will enable you to avoid producing a deliverable that totally misses the boat.

Here are some examples of what the conversation between Isabel and Steven might have sounded like had she asked for help at the outset.

---

1. BE PROACTIVE

- Steven, I'm happy to write a business plan. However, I've never written one before.
- That sounds like a good plan. I've never written a business plan before, however. Can we find some time to sit down and talk about what you're looking for?
- Yes, I'll absolutely get started on that, but I'm going to need some guidance from you, as I've never written one before.
- I agree on the approach, but I'd like to bring in some folks to help me, as I've never done this before.

---

2. ASK FOR RESOURCES/GUIDANCE

- Do you have a specific template or format in mind for the business plan?
- Do you have any examples of a business plan I can take a look at?
- Can you think of anyone I might speak with to help?
- You mentioned Ethan wrote a business plan for the marketing group last year. I'm going to reach out to him to get his thoughts. How does that sound?

3. REQUEST FEEDBACK OR OFFER MILESTONES

- I'm going to put together a list of bullet points for you to sign off on before starting on a full draft.
- Why don't I put together an outline for you to review before I start a first draft?
- Are there one or two sections I should focus on first to make sure I'm moving in the right direction?
- I think the key sections are the executive-overview, financials, and operations sections. Do you agree?

Had Isabel used this action strategy, she and Steven could have avoided much frustration (on the part of Isabel), disappointment (on the part of Steven), and wasted time (for both).

Jane Bellow, AEK Industries Summer Intern

Even though Isabel had never before written a business plan, she understood the concept. If the task at hand is an entirely unfamiliar concept, however, you're going to need to ask for clarification up front.

Jane Bellow was a summer intern with AEK Industries in Sweden. The first day on the job, her manager sat her down and told her she'd be working on buzz metrics. Jane had no earthly idea what buzz metrics were. Tongue-tied and confused, Jane sat there in silence, nodding her head and accepting her new assignment. To her boss, she appeared calm and composed—fully understanding and capable of the assignment. Inwardly, however, Jane was bewildered. What the hell were buzz metrics? She prayed to the Google gods that she'd be able to find an answer online after their meeting.

Later that day, Jane found herself caught between a rock and hard place. She had played along and pretended she understood the assignment when she didn't. Given that it was her first day, she was (understandably) intimidated and felt that asking for help out of the box would have sent up a red flag. Unfortunately, Jane was left to her own devices to figure it out. She certainly couldn't walk back into her boss's office and explain that, actually, she had no idea what buzz metrics were.

Here's some example language Jane could have used to ask for clarification on what buzz metrics were before using the rest of the action strategy to get the help she needed to do the job well.

ASK FOR CLARIFICATION

- I've actually never heard the term *buzz metrics* before. Would you mind defining it for me please?
- When you refer to *buzz metrics,* are you talking about standard marketing metrics or something different?
- Can you please elaborate on what exactly you mean by *buzz metrics*? That's a new term for me.
- I don't exactly understand what you mean by *buzz metrics.*

The Smart Ask, Part II

You won't always realize right away you need help on an assignment. It's not uncommon to find yourself halfway through a project before hitting a roadblock or starting to stumble. When that happens, it's equally important to ask for and get the help you need, keeping in mind two key goals:

1. Demonstrate how you've made progress to date; and
2. Show how you think you should move the ball forward.

The goal is to avoid asking "What should I do?" That question doesn't show you to be smart, thoughtful, qualified, or capable. Rather, it makes it seem as though you have nothing to contribute.

Instead, take a stand and put your stake in the ground. Given that you've been working on the project, show your boss that you've had a chance to think through your particular problem and offer a suggestion on what to do. Then ask for thoughts or feedback on how to proceed. Starting off with your ideas about what to do is far more powerful and effective than simply asking for outright guidance.

Reva Patel, Thompson Reed

Reva Patel worked in human resources at Thompson Reed and was responsible for building out a professional development curriculum for high-potential employees at the company. Reva was working toward her Ph.D. in industrial organizational psychology and had consulted for leading financial services firms before joining Thomson Reed. Reva had always been a top performer and was considered an integral member of her team.

After the merger of Thomson and Reed in 2008, the combined company continued to make small acquisitions regularly. In early 2010, Reva was asked to create an orientation program to bring on board 150 employees from a recently acquired information-systems-platform company. Integration of new employees was never easy, and bringing so many people on board in one fell swoop had unique logistical and coordination challenges that Reva wondered if she could handle on her own.

Reva got off to a good start with the orientation program and was pleased with the progress of the technical training. However, planning the firm-wide business-overview sessions was another matter altogether. Reva was trying to get several business-unit heads to speak on a panel during orientation. Of the six department heads Reva had reached out to, only two had responded to her request to participate—and each had said no. As the clock continued to tick and the group's start date approached, she began to sweat.

Reva realized that she was probably going to need to ask her boss, Andrew, to intervene and reach out to the department heads directly to ask for their help. Growing more exasperated by the day, Reva finally approached Andrew and asked him what to do. Their conversation went something like this:

> *Andrew, I'm not sure what to do—I've reached out to six different business unit heads to speak at orientation and I haven't been able to confirm a single one.*
>
> *Two department heads said no, and the other four haven't responded yet.*
>
> *I recognize that everyone is busy, but it's really important that the new employees have an opportunity to get a meaningful overview of the firm, and the business heads are key to making that happen. What do you think I should do?*

Then, a funny thing happened. Reva's boss suggested he reach out directly to the remaining business-unit heads. Of course, this was the same course of action that Reva would have proposed had she thought to give an opinion rather than just ask for outright guidance. Unfortunately, Andrew didn't know that this was Reva's plan. He thought this was an original idea and that he was solving her problem for her.

It was an opportunity lost, for sure. Reva could have shown how capable she was, or that she was a good problem solver. She could have suggested Andrew reach out to the business-unit heads himself, making a strong case for why they would respond to him more readily than to her. Instead, Reva asked Andrew what to do and made it seem as though she couldn't think clearly under pressure.

———— • ————

When you are working on a project and find yourself stuck or needing some guidance, you typically have an idea of the direction to take. Rather than going in and asking for outright guidance about what to do, instead consider the following strategy to position yourself in a more favorable light.

The Strategy: The Smart Ask, Part II

1.   Start with what you know.
2.   State your intended direction.
3.   Ask for feedback/confirmation.

On-the-Job Case

1.   Start with What You Know

Andrew, we're making great progress on the orientation program and the technical training piece is shaping up nicely.

Unfortunately, I'm having difficulty getting the business-unit overview sessions scheduled.

Reva would have done much better for herself had she walked into Andrew's office and presented the issue clearly—she was in good shape with the technical training but was facing roadblocks with the business-unit heads.

Giving Andrew a clear idea of her progress to date would have positioned her in a positive light. Then she could have gone on to explain what was outstanding (the business-unit overviews), where or how she was struggling (no one wanted to participate), and what she needed help with (getting senior leadership on board with this important aspect of orientation).

2. State Your Intended Direction

I've reached out to six different department heads about their availability to participate in the sessions and I haven't received a single yes yet. I think it would be far more effective if you reached out directly and asked for their help. They'll have a much harder time saying no to you than they will to me.

As a smart, informed professional, you rarely have absolutely no idea whatsoever of what to do when problems arise. Typically you have some ideas to offer on the topic or you're able to come up with the pros and cons of various courses of action.

Reva approached Andrew with an open-ended plea

for help: "I don't know what to do, can you please help?" Ironically, she did have a pretty good idea about what to do, but she didn't let on to such. Reva knew the right course of action, she just didn't give herself enough credit.

It's always better to have an opinion and lay your stake in the ground than to come off as wishy-washy or uninformed. Give the problem some context, lay out the facts, and propose a couple of options that may work. If you're right, you'll look great. If you're wrong, at least you'll show that you're thoughtful and able to formulate your own ideas and possible solutions.

You undoubtedly sound more professional and better informed when you give someone an idea of the direction you think you should take and then ask for their confirmation or feedback versus asking them outright, "What should I do?" That question intimates that you haven't put any thought or effort into the situation (i.e., you're lazy) and/or implies that you're looking to someone else to solve your problem for you (i.e., you're inept).

The better approach is to think through several options and give your manager an idea of what might work. Demonstrate that you've put some thought into the issue; you've got good judgment and you're able to evaluate various options. While you're not *certain* of the right course of action, you're not completely in the dark either.

3.   Ask for Feedback/Confirmation

Do you agree with my approach or do you have another suggestion for handling this?

Instead of asking Andrew what to do, Reva should have shared her proposed course of action, then asked whether he agreed. Andrew and Reva *were* in agreement. The solution Andrew proposed (getting on the horn personally to rope his colleagues into participating) was the same solution Reva had envisioned.

No doubt Andrew would have thought more highly of Reva had she come to him with a proposed solution in hand versus a lazy "What should I do?" The example language below will give you an opportunity to lay your stake in the ground and then get thoughts, feedback, or clarification from your boss on your proposed plan of action.

Reva would have been far more successful in her conversation with Andrew by approaching him with some of the following example language.

---

1. START WITH WHAT YOU KNOW

- Andrew, we're making great progress on the orientation program, and the technical training piece is shaping up nicely. Unfortunately, I'm struggling to get the business-unit overview sessions scheduled.
- Andrew, I'd like to post you on orientation. We're in good shape on the technical training, which is great. I'm not having as much luck, however, with the business-unit overviews—no one has agreed to participate yet.

- Andrew, the orientation program is moving along. I have good news on the technical training side but not such good news regarding the business-unit heads.
- We're in good shape on orientation but I'm in need of some help with the business-unit heads. No one has committed yet. Do you have a few minutes to catch up?

2. STATE YOUR INTENDED DIRECTION

- I think it would be more effective if you reached out directly to ask for their participation. They'll have a harder time saying no to you than they will to me.
- I don't think I will get much further without bringing you in directly to encourage them to participate.
- You know I wouldn't ask if it wasn't urgent, but I need you to step in here and help out.
- I'm happy to draft a voice-mail script for you or send you an e-mail to forward along to them to make it as easy as possible for you.

3. ASK FOR FEEDBACK/CONFIRMATION

- What do you think of reaching out to them directly?
- Does that sound reasonable—or is there something else you'd suggest?
- Does that sound like a good plan of action?
- Do you agree with that approach or have any other suggestions?

It goes without saying that you're going to need help at some point on the job. There is absolutely nothing wrong with asking for help—you just have to do it in a smart way. Show how thoughtful you are and put your stake in the ground when you have some plausible ideas about the best course of action to take.

Using the GOTJ action strategies will ensure you get the resources you need to do your job well while positioning you as the on-top-of-it professional that you are.

TROUBLESHOOTING

Q: What if I really don't have any idea about the right course of action to take? *Then* can I ask "What should I do?"

A: Worst-case scenario: If you really don't know what to do, highlight that you've been thinking about the problem and let your manager know that you haven't been able to come up with a viable solution.

In essence, you're looking for an A for effort. Having shown your initiative and thoughtfulness, you can then say something like:

I REALLY DON'T KNOW WHAT TO DO. . . .

- I've been working hard on coming up with a couple of options, but I just can't seem to figure it out.
- I'm at a standstill here and I'm not sure how to proceed. I'd like to bring you into the process to help out.
- I feel like I've exhausted all of my options and I'm still coming up short. Can we sit down and talk about this?
- I've tried to come up with a solution but I don't think I'm going to get there on my own. Do you have some time to sit down and talk through some possible scenarios?

Q: Is it okay to ask someone junior to me for help? Should I worry about looking dumb in front of someone I'm supposed to be managing?

A: Yes, it is okay to ask people junior to you for help. You are paying them a compliment and letting them know that you value their judgment or input. Oftentimes, junior employees have great insight into how things get done, whom to go to when you need something, or what the fastest way to reach the boss is.

However, you need to be specific about what you need help with and why. In theory, you should only ask people junior to you for help on a particular aspect of an assignment that perhaps they are closer to and have more experience with. It should be something concrete and finite that you think they can help with, for instance:

- Chris, I'm working on putting together a project plan for Demetrius and I'm having some issues with the marketing section.
- I think you did something similar last year for Amanda. Do you have a template of the section that I could take a look at?

Instead of the following, which won't go over well:

- Hey, Chris, Demetrius [our boss] asked me to write up a project plan and I have no idea what to do. What do you think?

In the second scenario, Chris would probably wonder why the hell you're senior to him if you can't even write a project plan. Finally, keep in mind the "spread your questions" tip earlier in this chapter and make sure you're not always going to the same people for help, especially the more junior folks, or they may begin to talk.

Q: Why can't I just google "business plan" and figure out the answer online? Why even let on to my boss that I don't know how to do something?

A: Think of Jane at AKE Industries as your cautionary tale, stuck in Sweden agonizing about a task she doesn't know how to do. Using the "I'll google it" strategy runs the risk of not being able to find what you're looking for. Then you've got a bigger problem on your hands—you've got to go back to your boss or manager with your tail between your legs to admit that you don't really know what to do after all.

Q: What if I need help from someone who is aggressive or typically unsupportive?

A: Even if you work for a real a-hole, he or she will typically benefit from your doing your job well versus doing it poorly. You have to make the case that you need help so that you can do a good job for them— everyone's incentives should be aligned (in theory). You have to emphasize to your manager that investing five minutes up front (to give you some direction or help) will avoid five hours of wasted time on the back end in lost productivity.

Make this argument explicitly. Tell your boss that a few minutes of her time will enable you to do your job faster or better, freeing you up sooner to work on additional projects or freeing her up later on so that she won't have to waste time fixing your work.

If your manager is intimidating, acknowledge that you appreciate how valuable her time is. Then let her know that you're asking for guidance for precisely that reason—to do a good job the first time around and save everyone wasted time, energy, and resources (not to mention frustration).

Here are some ways to ask for help from someone intimidating or short on time:

- Daria, I know how busy you are, but I need five minutes of your time to talk about the plant improvements before I get started. I don't want to waste any time going down the wrong path.
- Luis, I want to make sure I'm moving in the right direction on the merchandising layout. It would be a huge help to talk through it quickly with you for a few minutes.
- Adam, I hate to ask, but I need five minutes of your time in the next day or so to review the regional strategy documents.
- Erica, is there any way you can squeeze me in today or tomorrow? I've got some outstanding questions on the floor-plan design that can't wait until next week. I'm worried if we don't talk soon, you won't have a chance to influence the process.

chapter six

Ask for Feedback

I'm not going to tell you everything is okay and allow you to be mediocre. I played [football] for a long time; the coaches that drive me crazy to this day are the ones that told me I was good all the time. "Well, hey, you're doing a great job," and I knew I was mediocre as hell. And the guy that was on my ass that made me be good every day is the guy that I appreciate right now.

—Jason Garrett, interim coach of the
Dallas Cowboys

Jeff Jenkins, Investment Banking Analyst

Jeff Jenkins was a first-year banking analyst who was technically proficient beyond anyone's wildest dreams—he was *the* analyst every vice president wanted staffed on their deals. Jeff stopped by his vice president Karen's office one evening after finishing an important client meeting and asked how she thought he had done presenting his merger analysis. In truth he had done a lousy job. While Jeff could build a cash-flow model faster than Karen could say the very words, he wasn't good at explaining his technical analysis to a nonnumbers audience, i.e., the client.

In an ideal world, Karen would have sat down with Jeff and told him that while he did a great job putting together the analysis, he needed to work on his client-presentation skills. She would have praised his accuracy and facility with numbers, but would have let him know that he needed to work on turning his technical analysis into language easily understandable and accessible to a layperson. She would have told him to speak with Brian, another analyst who was particularly good at this, or would have spent time going through the presentation with him and showing him the ways in which she would have presented the numbers differently.

Unfortunately for Jeff, it was 9:30 p.m. and Karen was racing to get home. She told Jeff he did a great job and thanked him for his hard work. Karen knew she was robbing Jeff of invaluable feedback, but two things were working against both of them at that moment. One, Karen was exhausted and wanted to end her day. Two, Karen hadn't had time to think about delivering a message that would be helpful and constructive. Instead, she punted—to avoid a difficult conversation and to save time.

———— • ————

How many times have you inquired about your own performance or been in a situation where someone has asked you how they were doing, only to answer or to hear, "You're doing a great job." You walk away relieved, but also somewhat unconvinced—knowing on some level perhaps that the other person may not have given you the whole truth.

It's not uncommon to drop by someone's office or corner a colleague directly following a meeting to ask, "How did I do?" or "How do you think that memo looked that just went out to the client?" While asking for some informal or in-the-moment feedback after an important meeting or at the end of a major project may seem like a smart thing to do, in truth it's generally ineffective.

Create Mentoring Opportunities

- *By soliciting feedback, you acknowledge that you value the other person's judgment and opinion.*
- *The message you convey is "You have wisdom to impart" and "I'm open to self-improvement."*
- *Oftentimes, this dynamic can serve as the beginning of an invaluable mentor/mentee relationship.*

I spend a good deal of time in front of corporate and business school audiences presenting the Great on the Job strategies. I also spend a lot of time asking for and analyzing reviews and feedback on the course. I do something else too. About halfway through every presentation, I call on an un-suspecting audience member and ask him how I'm doing.

Guess what people say? To this day, I've never gotten a bad review. Good for me. As much as I like to think that each and every person who sits through a Great on the Job presentation finds the material as powerful and helpful as I do, I do know better. I'm usually at about a 90 percent suc-cess rate in people's reviews of my presentations. But when I call on you in front of a room full of people, 100 percent of the time you'll tell me I'm doing a great job.

Who can blame you? I've just called you out in front of over a hundred people and asked for some feedback on the spot. I didn't give you a heads-up. I didn't pull you aside before the presentation to let you know that I might want some feedback along the way and ask that you please pay attention to some aspect of the presentation.

I didn't do myself any favors either. If that spontaneous, on-the-spot, in-front-of-a-hundred-plus-people feedback were the only feedback I solicited, you can imagine I'd have a hard time continuously improving my content.

Here's the deal—feedback can't be asked for on the spot. Feedback is a tool that can make you better at your job, but it has to be given and received with anticipation. It is also not to be given in a public forum. Feedback should be asked for or offered off-line and behind closed doors, period. Giving someone your thoughts on how they're doing in front of others, no matter how well-intentioned you are or how timely the comments may be, is a bad idea. Absolutely no one can be expected to effectively receive constructive criticism in front of others.

Let's revisit the situation with our banking analyst Jeff and his VP Karen.

1. Jeff worked on some technical analysis for Karen and did a good job.
2. Jeff presented this technical analysis to the client and didn't do a good job.
3. Jeff asked Karen how he did presenting to the client.
4. Karen lied and told him he did a great job.

What went wrong? Jeff's on-the-spot and after-the-fact inquiry didn't give Karen the time to collect her thoughts to prepare or deliver honest and thoughtful feedback. It was a lose-lose situation for Jeff and Karen, with both of them at fault.

———— • ————

There are two overriding goals of getting constructive feedback—they are both equally important and neither trumps or negates the other:

1. Make the feedback as useful as possible to you.
2. Make the request as easy as possible on the person giving the feedback.

Goal #1: Make the Feedback as Useful as Possible to You

As evidenced by Jason's Garrett's experience as an NFL player and Jeff Jenkins's experience as a superstar technical analyst, getting positive feedback isn't the goal. Getting useful, helpful, actionable feedback is.

Hearing you're doing a great job when you're in fact doing a mediocre or subpar job is, at best, a minor disservice and, at worst, a grand injustice to you. No one cares more about managing your career than you do. If everyone tells you you're doing a great job, but year-end review time comes and it turns out that everyone was just being nice, well, you're the one up sh*t's creek, not the folks who cheered you on disingenuously.

So how do you get useful, helpful, actionable feedback? It starts with planting a seed in advance, making your request specific, and soliciting concrete and actionable ideas for improvement—we'll take a look at each one in detail shortly.

Goal #2: Make the Request as Easy as Possible on the Person Giving the Feedback

No less important than making the feedback useful to you is making the process as easy and painless as possible on the person giving the feedback. Asking someone to give you feedback on your performance requires an investment of their time, energy, and resources with the express purpose of advancing *your* career or professional development.

While the benefits of feedback go both ways (improving your performance should ultimately benefit your manager, colleagues, and organization), you should by all means be extremely considerate of the time and energy required of your manager or colleagues to provide you with cogent, helpful feedback.

Be generous by making your request in advance, scheduling the session around the other person's calendar, and, most important, giving your reviewer some direction on what concrete areas of performance you're looking for feedback on.

The Strategy

Phase I: The Preparation

1. Plant the seed.
2. Schedule the conversation.
3. Provide specific guidance (of what you're looking for).

On-the-Job Case

1. Plant the Seed

Karen, I'd love to get some feedback on my presentation after our client meeting next week. Could we find a time to talk after the meeting?

One of the most important aspects of asking for feedback is giving someone a heads-up. Let people know at the outset of a project that you're open to, and interested in, getting feedback. That puts others on notice and gives them an opportunity to prepare and collect their thoughts over time.

Planting a seed also improves your chances of the feedback actually being useful and constructive. Giving someone time to think about your performance in advance opens the door for an honest and constructive conversation.

2. Schedule the Conversation

Karen, I'd love to schedule a feedback session as we discussed. Could you please let me know a couple of times that work for you in the next few weeks? I will happily work around your schedule.

You've asked for the feedback, now you need to make it happen. Don't wait for your supervisor to schedule the conversation, and don't assume that he or she will take the lead in making the feedback session happen. It is your

Let's Do Lunch

Feedback can be exchanged over coffee or lunch outside the office, but only if you think the person giving the feedback has the time and/or will enjoy the break.

If your supervisor is always pressed for time and never takes a lunch break, assume that proposing a lunchtime feedback session out of the office is only going to make the process that much more stressful or unappealing to her.

responsibility to make sure this conversation is put on the calendar.

Be as accommodating as possible in finding a time that works on her calendar or fits into her schedule. The easier you make it on the other person, the more likely it is the dialogue will actually take place.

3. Provide Specific Guidance (of What You're Looking For)

I'm working hard on communicating in a nontechnical way, so I'd be particularly interested in your thoughts on how effective I've been in this area.

All of the advance notice in the world and thoughtful scheduling around your manager's calendar won't make any difference if you don't give the person a set of specific questions or topics you'd like to discuss in advance.

Be clear about what you'd like feedback on. Are you looking for your manager's thoughts on how you're managing your workload, keeping a project on time and on budget, or interacting with suppliers and vendors? Or would you like feedback on dealing with customer requests, drafting press releases for product launches, or designing workshop sessions? Whatever you are interested in learning more about, be clear from the start.

This concept of providing specific prompts for your manager goes back to the multiple-choice strategy in Chapter 3, "Be Strategically Proactive." When you simply ask your manager a lazy, open-ended question about how you're doing, she may not comment on your area of specific concern. Asking pointed questions about specific projects or areas of your performance will give her something to react to or something substantive to discuss. It will also make it easier for her—she won't have to conjure up discussion points because you'll have done much of the prep work for her.

This step of the process is easily done via e-mail—sending a quick note with the topics or bullet points you'd like to discuss will likely give your boss a good starting point from which to craft her thoughts or message in a constructive way.

———— • ————

Let's take a look at our example language to see what Jeff could have done differently to plan for and ensure a productive feedback session with Karen.

1. PLANT THE SEED

- Karen, I'd love to get some feedback on my presentation after our client meeting next week. Could we find a time to talk afterwards?
- This is going to be my first merger transaction and I'd appreciate your opinion and feedback on how I do as we go through the process.

- Would it be possible to sit down with you once we're under way with the project to get some feedback on how I'm doing?
- Karen, I'd love to hear your thoughts on my client presentation. How about scheduling a feedback session sometime after the meeting?

2. SCHEDULE THE CONVERSATION

- Karen, I'd love to schedule a feedback session as we discussed. Could you please let me know a couple of times that work for you in the next few weeks? I will work around your schedule.
- Pedro, I know we spoke last month about getting some feedback. Could we go ahead and schedule a time to discuss?
- Hi, Mehta, I just wanted to stop by to see if you had any time in the next few weeks to sit down and do a feedback session on my management of the young-leadership event?
- Now that we're about halfway through the focus-group sessions, I was wondering if we could set up a time for me to get some feedback from you?

3. PROVIDE SPECIFIC GUIDANCE (OF WHAT YOU'RE LOOKING FOR)

- I'm working hard on communicating in a non-technical way and I'm interested in your thoughts on how effective I've been in this area.
- I'd like to know how I'm doing managing the clients' expectations, connecting with my audience, and handling Q and A.
- I'd like to know what you think about my work organizing the speakers and panelists for next month's leadership summit.
- What, if any, additional areas of development do you think I should focus on?

Jeff needed to let Karen know in advance that he wanted feedback so that she would have a heads-up to prepare her thoughts. Karen would have been better equipped to give Jeff some meaningful feedback regarding his presentation skills, and the advance notice would have helped avoid the late-night encounter that forced Karen to punt and tell Jeff all was well.

———— • ————

Okay, let's assume you've properly set up your feedback session. Now you've got to be equally diligent about preparing for the actual conversation. The goal of Phase II is to have a productive conversation and milk your reviewer for all she's worth in actionable tips, strategies, and advice to improve your performance. Get her thoughts on building relationships, managing teams, beefing up your skill set, or anything else you should be doing to push yourself to new levels professionally.

The Strategy

Phase II: The Conversation

1. Ask for concrete ways to improve.
2. Say thank you.
3. Wait, digest, and revisit.

On-the-Job Case

1. Ask for Concrete Ways to Improve

I appreciate your candor. Do you have any specific thoughts on how I can improve my communication skills?

The most important thing to come out of a feedback session is the practical advice you receive from your supervisor or mentor. If Elliot tells you that you're not doing a good job, don't let him off the hook without some pointed questions about how you can improve your performance. Do you need different assignments to work on or should you spend more time working on the ones you already have? If you didn't deliver on results, what are some ways you can improve your sales leads? If your marketing campaign fell on deaf ears, what can you do to make sure the same thing doesn't happen next time?

This is the time for flattery, as in, "I really value your opinion and I'd love to know your thoughts on how I can improve my performance."

Ask for suggestions of whom to speak with, how to improve, what to do, what not to do, how to engage your teammates or client differently or more energetically—now is the time to ask those questions and get all of the input you can.

2. Say Thank You

Thanks much for taking the time to sit down with me this afternoon. I really appreciate your willingness to share your thoughts.

It feels great to get positive feedback—if you typically hear positive things from your manager and colleagues, good for you, you're on the right track. The goal, however, is continuous improvement and learning, not just feeling good. If you have a tough feedback session, remind yourself that the *goal of the session is not to make you feel good. The goal is to make you better at your job.*

Take comfort in that you've just taken an important step toward improving your performance by addressing any bumps in the road. You are making an investment in your career. Even if the feedback is hard to take, hopefully it's helpful and constructive.

With that in mind, try to be as gracious as possible in receiving the feedback and be conscious of thanking your boss for his time and thoughtfulness. Then, think about what you can do differently going forward.

3. Wait, Digest, and Revisit

I'd like to think through all of this and come back to you with some additional questions if that's all right?

Hopefully, your feedback session goes well and you take away some valuable pointers and counsel. You have a sense of what you need to do to take your performance to the next level, and you feel ready and able to make positive changes toward reaching your professional goals.

However, if the conversation does not go well, then step number 3 becomes *very* important. Whatever you do, no matter the circumstances, don't lose your cool. If you are upset, get out of your building as quickly as possible to let off some steam. Take a walk, call a friend (on your mobile and out of earshot of your colleagues having lunch), or have a good cry. Just don't have the emotional outburst in front of your colleagues.

Emotional outbursts of any kind should be bottled up and saved for the bathroom stall on the floor below you or the deli across the street. It is supremely unprofessional to lose it in front of colleagues, and the outburst will be no doubt be remembered long after the actual content of the review has been forgotten.

That said, you don't have to be disingenuous. It's okay to acknowledge disappointment or surprise (as you'll see in the example language that follows). Just take a deep breath and politely excuse yourself. Then take twenty-four hours to digest the information.

Once you've removed yourself from the stressful situation, think with a clear head about the feedback and evaluate (more objectively now) whether it was fair or accurate. The goal is to remove your initial reaction of shock, disappointment, or anger from the conversation and turn the criticism into constructive action items (think about step 1—ask for concrete ways to improve) and follow up on the conversation the next day once the dust has settled to ask for clarification, to argue your case, or to dig deeper to get to the bottom of the disagreement.

———— • ————

The actual conversation should start with the typical niceties of any interaction in which someone is helping you (e.g., *Thank you so much for sitting down with me today. I really appreciate it and I'm eager to hear your thoughts*). Express appreciation that the other person is taking time out of his or her busy schedule to give you feedback. Here's some example language for each of the steps for how the conversation may transpire.

---

1. ASK FOR CONCRETE WAYS TO IMPROVE

- I appreciate your candor. Do you have any specific thoughts on how I can improve my communication skills?
- How would you suggest I change the introduction and Q-and-A sections next time to reflect

---

your comment that they felt rushed and somewhat incomplete?

- How would you recommend getting the R-and-D team on board earlier in the process next time?
- Is there anyone here who you think does a particularly good job drafting scopes of work? I'd love to get some ideas from them.

2. SAY THANK YOU

- Thanks much for taking the time to sit down with me this afternoon. I really appreciate your willingness to share your thoughts.
- I absolutely understand your points and I'm going to spend some time thinking about ways to improve on the areas you mentioned. Thank you again.
- That's an interesting way of thinking about things—I hadn't considered that angle, thank you for bringing it to my attention.
- I'm not sure I completely understand or agree with all of your points, but I do appreciate your taking the time to sit down with me. Thank you..

3. WAIT, DIGEST, AND REVISIT

- I'd like to think through all of this and come back to you with some additional questions if that's all right?
- Would it be okay if I took a few days to think about your comments and schedule a follow-up discussion?
- You've given me a lot to think about and I'd like to continue the conversation after I have some more time to reflect on all of this.
- I'm sure I'm going to have some additional thoughts and questions as I digest all of this information. Would you be willing to have a follow-up conversation?

Just like asking for help, asking for feedback can be an effective tool for improving performance. But feedback is like a precious gem—it needs to be mined. Seldom do people find diamonds and sapphires just lying around the surface. You've got to really dig deep to find those gems.

Furthermore, don't assume all is well just because you haven't heard otherwise. Take ownership of the process by initiating the dialogue, making sure the conversation happens, and providing ample guidance to your boss or colleagues so that they can give constructive and effective feedback on areas of performance that you care about and that matter.

TROUBLESHOOTING

Q: How often should I ask for feedback?

A: As a general rule, getting feedback once a year is too little, and asking for feedback once a month is too often—and onerous. Think about creating opportunities to gauge your performance three to four times a year—quarterly is a good target. Also consider spreading your requests around—getting feedback three to four times a year might include talking to your mentor quarterly or asking a few different people how you're doing once a year.

If you're in a summer internship, try to create two to three touch points over the summer, asking for feedback at the midway and end points and also on an as-needed basis if certain projects or teams warrant it.

Q: How do I get feedback about whether people like me?

A: If you're looking for feedback on behavioral topics (e.g., how am I perceived around the office? Do people like working with me?) tread carefully—feedback shouldn't be used to gauge popularity.

That said, being well liked shouldn't be underestimated. If you wonder what your colleagues really think about you, ask these types of questions that speak to your reputation as a team player:

- How do you think I did managing team morale on the Red Bull print campaign?
- Do people consider me a team player?
- I try hard to keep everyone in the loop and share credit with the junior team. How do you think I'm doing on those fronts?
- I'm working hard to soften my image and not be so hard-driving. Am I still being perceived as working people too hard?

Q: How do I get feedback from people junior to me?

A: People working for you can often give valuable and constructive feedback about how you or your teams can work better, faster, or smarter. Getting feedback not just from your superiors but also from subordinates shows people who work for you that you value their opinions and care about continuous improvement.

An effective way to encourage someone junior to you to give you real and meaningful feedback is to make the feedback session mutual—ask for their thoughts on how you're doing and simultaneously offer to give them some feedback on their performance.

By making it mutual, you give your subordinates permission to give you honest and constructive feedback because they know you are going to do the same for them. Model good behavior by setting up the conversation in advance and following the steps laid out in this chapter—and you'll encourage your subordinates to do the same thing for you.

Q. How do I get feedback from someone who insists all the time I'm doing a great job?

A: You have two options here. The first is to ask again; the second is to find someone new to ask. If you opt to ask again, consider using a "leading question" the second time around and bring up instances in which you think your work could have used some improvement. Offer up your honest assessment of a particular situation, and ask your supervisor if she agrees with your assessment. You'll be more likely to hear honest feedback using this approach, but be mindful of the phrasing you use. It's important to not lean too far toward the negative. Think along these lines:

- I appreciate that you think I'm doing a great job, but I actually think I have some room to improve, and I'd like your thoughts.

  Not these:

- I think I did a terrible job handling the publicity debacle and I'd like to know your thoughts on how I can improve my work.

  Your modus operandi should be that your performance is or has been adequate but you're looking for excellence. Your baseline isn't failure, but it may be mediocrity (at worst). Assume you're operating at a baseline of adequacy and then demonstrate your willingness and desire to be even better. Don't suggest that you did a terrible job or think something was a total failure—you'll just give your manager free rein to agree and tell you how awful your performance was. Instead, point to specific tasks and projects and acknowledge room for improvement.

Here is some additional example language you can use in this kind of conversation.

DO SAY	DON'T SAY
I think that meeting could have been more productive. Do you have thoughts on how I can keep people on track next time?	I know that meeting was a disaster. Do you have any thoughts on how I can keep people on track more effectively next time?
I recognize that the report had some holes in it. Do you have any suggestions on how to tie the conclusions together better next time?	I know the report looked terrible. What should I do differently next time?
I know there's room for improvement in my speaking skills. Do you have any tips?	I sounded awful with the sales team. What did you think?

Q. What should I do about negative feedback I don't agree with?

A: If you don't think you're getting fair or reasonable feedback, you are absolutely entitled to push back on your supervisor. Be mindful of the twenty-four-hour rule and be sure to have the conversation in an objective way; you don't want to be argumentative or confrontational. Think about graciously proving others wrong.

The way to do that is to look for anecdotal evidence or examples to support your cause. Talk to some additional colleagues or teammates to get their opinions. You want to be able to confirm or deny a pattern; if everyone says the same thing about your producing sloppy work, then the feedback is probably valid. If you hear from several other people that this is not the case, you may have grounds to go back to your manager and argue your case or cite evidence to the contrary.

If you have concrete examples showing that the negative feedback was unfair or wrong, by all means feel free to share it. If your manager knocks you for not following up on an outstanding purchase order and you have an e-mail showing that you reached out to the supplier but never heard back, then go ahead and forward the e-mail with a quick note explaining that the communication had in fact taken place. Don't be mean or aggressive or say, "I told you so"—just be professional and to the point and let him know you did indeed follow up.

If others say you've produced excellent, not sloppy,

work, then go ahead and schedule a follow-up meeting with your boss to revisit the issue. Let him know that you take his feedback seriously and you work hard to produce great results—which is why you sought out additional feedback from peers and colleagues after your disappointing review with him. Point to the contrary evidence that shows you did great work for others on your team or within the organization, and show him that you care about improvement—how can you do the same for him? Do the two of you need to communicate better, coordinate better, or does he need to more clearly lay out his expectations so that you can meet or exceed them? Have an open dialogue to find some common ground about how you can excel for him just as you've been doing for others.

Q: I've been working on a project and I just realized that I should probably get some feedback on it. I'm almost done and I know I should have asked earlier. Is it too late?

A: You can still use the same two-phase GOTJ action strategy but in a more condensed manner. You still can and should plant the seed—meaning, don't ask for feedback on the spot. Instead, acknowledge that although you're halfway through or finished with a project, you'd love to get some feedback on how things went (or are going).

Ask your manager if he's open to providing some feedback, then go ahead and schedule a conversation in the near term to discuss your performance. Be sure to send him your questions or areas of interest in advance.

In effect, you're doing the same thing as you would at the outset of a project, you're just starting the whole process at a midway or end point, meaning your manager may have to approach the conversation retroactively to come up with feedback.

Q: I'm dreading the conversation. Can I skip the face-to-face meeting and just ask my mentor or manager to e-mail me his thoughts on how I'm doing?

A: It may be tempting, but the answer is no—you can't exchange feedback via e-mail. Going back to our discussion in Chapter 2, "The Foolproof Download," contentious or potentially contentious issues must be handled in person—tone and tenor get lost and people often misinterpret information delivered electronically. You're just going to have to gather your nerve and ask to have the conversation in person. That said, the in-person feedback session is much better anyway—it's certainly more gratifying to hear positive news in person. Conversely, if the feedback isn't stellar, then you'll be able to ask questions on the spot to clarify points, highlight inaccuracies, or just emphasize that you're committed to self-improvement. You wouldn't be able to do any of that over e-mail.

Again, the only exception to the rule is that step 3, provide specific guidance (of what you're looking for), can be done via e-mail. It's often easier to e-mail your boss a list of topics or areas you'd like feedback on once you've planted the seed and then gone ahead and scheduled the discussion. Sending bullet points of areas you hope to discuss will give your boss a starting point from which to craft his thoughts or message in a constructive way.

part three

---

stay out of trouble

chapter seven

Answer Questions (You Don't Know the Answers To)

Nobody knows everything, but everybody knows something.

—WIKIPEDIA SLOGAN

How many times have you been asked a question that you don't know the answer to and wished that the person had just asked you this other question instead—the one you were ready and waiting for, the one you had a great answer to? Doesn't it always seem that you can come up with a perfectly plausible, authoritative, convincing, or smart answer after the fact? Yet in the moment you get flustered, tripped up on the details, or simply fixate on the one piece of information you don't actually know. Sadly, you fail to convey that sense of competence or confidence that you typically demonstrate, all because you simply didn't know *that* answer.

There's not a soul alive who's *never* been put on the spot or who has *always* had the right answer (perhaps your boss seems to live under that lucky star, but it's a rare breed indeed). Whether the question you're asked is as simple as "Where is Jonathan?" as technical as "What is the ad-spending increase at Real Simple from Q3 to Q4, 2010?" or as open-ended as "What is the team's latest thinking on labor and cost inputs for the Milwaukee production plant?" there is a way to answer the question intelligently and capably.

Given how smart and competent you are, it's hard to believe that you have nothing of value to add to the conversation. Even when you don't have an answer or the exact information at hand, you typically have *something* to offer—a related piece of information, an anecdote, an idea or inkling about what the right answer might be.

Julianne Taylor, Production Assistant

Julianne Taylor was an production assistant at a small media firm in southern Florida. Julianne's boss, Dean, overheard Julianne on the phone one evening with a high-maintenance client, responding to an inquiry about who was going to be at an important meeting the next day. Dean's team hadn't yet finalized attendees because of conflicting travel schedules. Dean overheard the following:

> *Erin [client], I'm definitely going to be there. Dean won't be able to make it, because he's traveling tomorrow, but it will be either Andrew or Marcus along with myself. I will reach out to both of them this evening to confirm and will come back to you first thing tomorrow morning, if not sooner.*

Brilliant, thought Dean. The team still hadn't decided who would be attending the meeting, yet Julianne handled the conversation perfectly. She gave the client the information she knew—something to work with—then acknowledged the missing information and promised to get it ASAP.

Further, she made the client feel like a priority—Dean knew all too well that even a simple thing such as not knowing who would be at a meeting could be construed by a client as a slight, an indication that the client wasn't a high priority for Dean's firm or that Dean and his partners were focused on other high-paying, high-profile clients instead.

————— • —————

When it comes to answering a question you don't know the answer to, Julianne did exactly what you can and should do. It is arguably the most simple and eloquent of all the GOTJ strategies.

The Strategy

1. Here's what I know
2. Here's what I don't know
3. Here's how I'll figure it out

On-the-Job Case

Here's What I Know

Hi, Erin, thanks so much for calling. I will definitely be at the meeting. Dean is traveling tomorrow, so he won't be able to make it.

Wikipedia was built on the notion that nobody knows everything but everybody knows something. The same holds true for you. You're not expected to know everything, but you do know lots of things and you should have a good sense of what's going on around you. You wouldn't have that great job or internship or have made it through college if you weren't smart and capable and on the ball.

Yet life today is perhaps defined more than ever by information overload—data and information coming at us at 90 miles per hour from all different directions. You're constantly juggling more projects, teams, information, clients, and deliverables than you can possibly keep in your mind. So it can't be expected that you know everything. What is expected is that you know something.

Instead of shrugging your shoulders and saying "I don't know" or "I'm not sure," the next time someone asks you where Jonathan is or what the team's latest thinking is, provide some related information. Think about answering the question like this:

- Acknowledge that Jonathan hasn't been seen all morning, although admit you don't know where he is at the moment.
- Highlight what the meeting is about even if you don't know who is attending.
- Explain where the numbers are trending even if you don't have last week's exact figures.
- State whom you are planning to target in next week's mass mailing even if you don't have the logistics and details finalized.

In effect, give your manager or client something to work with—some background, context, related or tangential information—so that they know you're plugged in. Make it known that while you don't have the exact answer to the question, you do in fact have something of value to offer—you're not completely out to lunch.

Here's What I Don't Know

Andrew and Marcus are both trying to make it. However, I'm waiting for confirmation from them both as we speak.

After you've given your client or boss a little something to work with, then be transparent and admit that you don't know the answer or have that exact piece of information. Honesty is always appreciated. Bullshitting is not. Don't try to make something up if you really don't know the answer.

If you have a good reason for not knowing, go ahead and share it. Let me know that the information isn't readily available, your contact at the client hasn't returned your call, or you've been tied up all morning on another project. Give me additional information if it's helpful, but don't turn it into an excuse. Just be matter-of-fact and transparent—I don't have that information, however . . .

Here's How I'll Figure It Out

I will reach out to both of them this evening to confirm and will get back to you first thing tomorrow morning, if that's okay?

Let people know that you'd be happy (thrilled!) to go get the information they need. This is what most people want or expect of you anyway—to go get the information, find the answer, figure it out. Take the initiative to follow up and inquire about who is attending the meeting, when the presentation is scheduled for, or what the memo says about the product update. Be proactive and do whatever you need to fill in the missing pieces.

Here are some examples of how you can answer a question you don't know the answer to.

1. HERE'S WHAT I KNOW

- We're all looking forward to the meeting tomorrow. Unfortunately, Dean can't make it as he's traveling, but I will be there.
- Actually Jonathan has been gone all morning, which is unlike him.
- The meeting is going to focus on editorial content for the December newsletter.
- We're planning to target all small businesses in the greater St. Louis area with the mass mailing.

2. HERE'S WHAT I DON'T KNOW

- Andrew and Marcus are both trying to make it and I'm awaiting for confirmation from them both as we speak.

- I don't know where he is at the moment however.
- I don't think it's been decided who is writing the feature story yet.
- We don't yet have details finalized on how many newsletters will actually go out.

3. HERE'S HOW I'LL FIGURE IT OUT

- I will reach out to both of them this evening to confirm and will come back to you first thing tomorrow morning if that's okay.
- Let me check Jonathan's calendar and see if he was planning on being out of the office today.
- Let me reach out to the editorial staff and come back to you via e-mail.
- I should have all of the logistics and details ironed out by early next week. . . . . I'll circle back to you as soon as I have everything finalized.

Using this strategy, Julianne finessed the call skillfully and showed that she had her bases covered. She communicated what she knew, what she didn't know, and then committed to follow up with the client with an answer ASAP. Perhaps not an ideal situation, but she did the best she could with a high-maintenance client and imperfect information.

Peter Wright, Vice President, Consumer Products

Peter Wright was a senior vice president in the soup and sauces division at a leading consumer products company. Peter had profit-and-loss responsibility for dozens of product lines. Peter spent most of his time focused on consumer trends and high-level marketing efforts for his brands; seldom did he get into the nitty-gritty details of how his products were selling daily or weekly. Given Peter's broad responsibilities, he expected his brand and assistant brand managers to know more about the numbers than he did.

Occasionally, Peter inquired about a competing product's market share for a particular quarter or time period. He was always amazed when a young manager answered, "Hmm . . . I don't have that information" or "Sorry, Peter, I'm not sure."

Peter didn't expect his junior employees to know all of the numbers cold, but he did expect his brand managers to know more about their specific products than he did. He didn't need them to memorize facts or figures, but he did expect them to have an idea of how a product and its competitors were performing at any given time. He wanted his teams to have context around an issue and take initiative in finding information.

Would it be so hard, he thought to himself, for someone to tell him how the competing product was doing even without hard data? Suppose he stopped by someone's desk and asked, "Hi, Will, how are you? I was wondering how [competitor] Progresso Light is doing these days and where their latest market-share numbers are shaking out?"

Short of getting the answer he was looking for, Peter was nonetheless impressed when he got a response like this:

Hi, Peter, Progresso Light has been gaining share—it reached fourteen percent last month. I haven't checked the latest Nielsen numbers yet for the quarter. Let me go take a look and I'll shoot you an e-mail or drop by to give you the information.

Here are some additional ways to show context around an issue and demonstrate that you're in the know even when you don't have an exact answer.

---

1. HERE'S WHAT I KNOW

- Peter, you probably know that Progresso Light has been gaining share—it reached fourteen percent last month.
- The recent ad campaign has been really strong so I expect their numbers to be trending up significantly.
- Progresso Light has had its best year to date in terms of market share.
- Peter, they've had a great run over the past two months with the new ad campaign.

---

2. HERE'S WHAT I DON'T KNOW

- I don't have numbers for the most recent quarter, but I have a sense of where they'll come out.
- I want to say they're at fifteen percent this month but I'm not one hundred percent sure. I'll know more next week.
- I actually don't have the quarterly data, unfortunately.
- I don't know the exact numbers for the quarter, Nielsen hasn't published them yet.

3. HERE'S HOW I'LL FIGURE IT OUT

- Let me go take a look at the latest figures and shoot the numbers over to you. Is there anything else you need?
- I will reach out to Caitlin and e-mail you as soon as I hear back from her.
- Let me go back and crunch some numbers for you and I'll get you the answer by the end of the day.
- I expect to have better numbers next week so I'll come back to you as soon as I have a definite answer.

Even though he didn't have the exact answer Peter was looking for, Will showed that he was capable of having an intelligent and somewhat informed conversation.

Will explained that Progresso Light was gaining share because of a promising ad campaign, then promised to go ahead and get the market share data for Peter ASAP.

That may have been all that Peter was looking for in the first place. It's not unheard of for a senior executive to stop by to talk to a junior employee just for kicks. Peter might have posed a question merely as an excuse to initiate a conversation with Will or to get a chance to know him. Peter may simply have been making small talk or just testing out Will's interpersonal skills—did he cave under pressure or take it in stride when the bigwig dropped by his desk to ask for an update?

Katherine Hsu, Business Development Manager

Katherine Hsu, a business development manager at a health-care services provider, was invited by her senior manager, Keith, to two meetings with strategic partners— Ortho Peeds and Stent Health. Katherine made it to the Ortho Peeds meeting but missed the Stent Health meeting because of a last-minute issue she had to attend to. The Ortho Peeds meeting went well, and the two companies planned to sign a memorandum of understanding (MOU) to begin exploring areas of collaboration— Katherine would be leading the charge.

Keith's boss, George, the director of corporate partnerships, stopped by Katherine's office that week to find out how the Stent Health meeting went. Katherine was ready to tell George all about the successful meeting with Ortho Peeds until she realized he wanted to know about the *other* meeting, the one she had missed with Stent Health.

Katherine maintained her composure and used the GOTJ strategy to put in a plug about some good news she did know related to her own work:

> *Hi, George, great to see you. Actually, I was at the Ortho Peeds meeting this week, which went great. We're moving forward with an MOU to collaborate.*
>
> *Unfortunately, I didn't make it to the Stent Health meeting—I got caught up with an emergency project and couldn't slip away. I heard the meeting went well, but I don't have further details.*
>
> *Keith was there, however. Why don't I go ahead and shoot you an e-mail or drop by as soon as I connect with him to give you an update?*

Here's some additional language Katherine could have used with George in response to his inquiry.

---

1. HERE'S WHAT I KNOW

- Hi, George, great to see you. Actually, I was at the Ortho Peeds meeting this week, which went great.
- We're close to signing an MOU and I'm excited to lead the charge.
- George, we actually had a great meeting with Ortho Peeds this week, but I missed the Stent Health meeting.
- George, as luck would have it, I only managed to make it to the Ortho Peeds meeting this week.

---

2. HERE'S WHAT I DON'T KNOW

- I didn't make it to the Stent Health meeting—I got caught up on an internal issue here and couldn't slip away.
- I was actually out of the office for personal reasons so I couldn't make the meeting.
- I wound up helping Erica finish up a speech at the last minute so I wasn't able to make the meeting.
- I heard Stent Health went well but I don't actually have any details.

3. HERE'S HOW I'LL FIGURE IT OUT

- Keith was there. Let me reach out to him to find out how it went and I'll come back to you with more details shortly.
- I haven't had a chance to circle up with Keith yet regarding Stent Health, but I've got a call in to him. As soon as I get an update, I will give you a call or stop by.
- I heard the Stent Health meeting went well but I don't have further details. Why don't I go ahead and shoot you an e-mail or drop by as soon as I connect with Keith to give you an update?
- I'm happy to go get some information for you and report back what I learn.

In all three cases, Julianne, Will, and Katherine used the three-step strategy to convey similar messages of being on top of it. Julianne finessed a potentially tricky conversation with a client. Will showed Peter that he was plugged in and capable of responding intelligently in the face of missing information. And Katherine took advantage of an opportunity to lob in a personal plug while answering a question she didn't have the answer to.

In each case, the three-step response of "Here's what I know," "Here's what I don't know," and "Here's how I'll figure it out" enabled the employees to put a better foot forward than if they'd simply answered, "I don't know."

The moral of the story is that you don't have to get tripped up by a question that stumps you. Keep your cool and remember that you're smart, you're in control, and you're on the ball. You may not have all the answers or information, but you probably have something relevant to offer.

TROUBLESHOOTING

Q: Can I flip-flop the strategy and start with what I don't know, move on to what I do know, and then go figure it out (steps 2-1-3)?

A: In an ideal world, you'd always start with the positive (here's what I know) before moving to the negative (here's what I don't know) and then finishing up again with the positive (here's how I'll figure it out). The idea of "sandwiching" the bad news between the good news ensures that you start off and end on a solid footing. Nonetheless, it's not always possible.

The second-best option is to acknowledge up front the information you don't have, soften the blow by adding "Here's what I know" next, and then quickly move on to go get the information you don't have. For instance, when George asked Katherine how the Stent Health meeting went, it wouldn't have been terrible for her to respond with the following:

George, I actually wound up missing the Stent Health meeting due to some urgent business here in the office. However . . .

I did make it to Ortho Peeds, which went really well. We're moving forward with the MOU and I'm going to be leading the charge.

Let me go reach out to Keith to get some additional information for you on the Stent Health meeting.

Q: What if my boss has no time or interest in the "Here's what I know part?" What if I work for a tough cookie and I know that this strategy simply won't work?

A: Inevitably, some people won't have the time or the patience to listen to the related information you have to share. If you're dealing with someone short on time or with a quick temper, then move straight to step two, acknowledge quickly that you don't have that information, and promise to go get it right away.

Q: What if I really should know the answer but I don't?

A: The best thing you can do in this situation is tell the truth—acknowledge that you should know the answer but don't. Be transparent and apologetic and then go get the answer. Some helpful to language to use includes:

I REALLY SHOULD KNOW BUT I DON'T

- I really should know the answer to your question, but I don't. Let me go make a few calls and get back to you.
- You know, I've been meaning to look into that and I haven't had any time to follow up. Let me go spend some time on it now, and I'll follow up with you by the end of the day.
- That's a great question and I can't believe I don't have an answer for you. Let me go find out for you.
- You know, I thought I had that information, but it turns out I don't. Would you mind if I came back to you on that?

Q: What if I have no idea what else to say when someone asks me a question? What kind of "related information" is fair game?

A: Some ideas of related information that may be of value or interest to someone include:

- An idea or inkling of what an answer or number might be (I have a sense, I think, I believe . . .)
- A related current event (I don't have our numbers yet from the charity auction, but I'm headed to the juvenile-diabetes fund-raiser tonight and I'm anxious to see how their crowd compares to ours).
- A note about your competition (I don't know where she's working, but I do know that Sterling Cooper just hired Dawn Fremont away from BBDO).
- A relevant article or news item (I haven't talked to Jim, but did you see his firm in Crain's business this morning?)
- An anecdote (that's funny you ask, I was just reading Chris Matthews's op-ed in the *Times* today and he talked about the same thing).

Q: What if I think I know an answer but I'm not 100 percent sure?

A: In this case, you want to state your position but also give yourself some cushion by admitting that you're not 100 percent certain. You can do this with the following three steps:

1. Put a "soft" stake in the ground—i.e., give yourself some wiggle room. Go on record as having an idea but not being certain.
2. Use a "hedge" to give yourself an opportunity to back down from your position in case you turn out to be wrong.

3. Ask for an opportunity to go double-check, confirm, revisit an issue, do whatever you need to do to get you from 50 percent or 75 percent certainty to 100 percent.

Here is some example language to use when you're not positive about an answer.

---

1. PUT A SOFT STAKE IN THE GROUND

- I think, I believe, I'm pretty sure . . . Adam and his team are flying out to CA tomorrow.
- Steve mentioned that . . . Progresso Light's market share was stronger than expected.
- My sense is, my understanding is, my hunch is . . . that we'll be starting the sale next week.
- Based on an initial review, yesterday's meeting, Elizabeth's comments . . . I'm putting our number in at eighty percent completion.

---

2. HEDGE

- I'll feel more comfortable giving you a final answer once I get the April report.
- I'll be better able to give you my recommendation once we've had a chance to circle back with Allison's team.

- Pending one final review of the numbers, I'll have better information.
- Until the meeting next Tuesday, I won't have full information.

3. MOVE FORWARD

- Let me go ahead and reach out to Stephanie one last time to confirm.
- I'd like to spend some time revisiting the situation this week before coming back to you with a final answer.
- Why I don't review the memo one last time before sending it off to Andrew for final sign-off?
- Let me reach out to Seth's team to verify the information.

chapter eight

Raise a Red Flag

Problems don't age well.

—Jamie Dimon, Chairman and CEO,
JPMorgan Chase (on *Charlie Rose*)

Steven Mong, Management Consultant

Steven Mong was a junior management consultant working on a supply-chain-optimization project for retailer Hipster, which was looking to increase productivity at a manufacturing plant in Europe.

Steven had spent several weeks building a financial model to gauge what impact different changes to schedule and labor would have on Hipster's capacity and output. Steven's manager, Ulrich, had sent over the analysis to the client in anticipation of a call the following day to discuss the team's recommendations.

Late that afternoon, as Steven was reviewing the slides in advance of the next day's call, he realized that one of the output pages was incorrect—it had pulled data from a previous model that didn't reflect the team's latest think-ing on labor costs.

Steven was devastated. He fixed the numbers and in-serted the correct output page into the presentation, but the client already had the wrong information. Should he just ignore the mistake and hope the client wouldn't notice? Or could he try to casually dismiss the mistake in the meeting if they did notice? That sounded somewhat appealing but risky.

Steven knew the numbers in the presentation were his sole responsibility. If the mistake was discovered by Ul-rich, Steven would look bad. If the mistake was discov-ered by the client, both Steven and Ulrich (and frankly, the whole firm) would look bad. Covering up or hiding behind the mistake seemed like a surefire way to just make matters worse.

Steven decided he was going to have to tell Ulrich about the mistake in advance of the meeting. Having cor-rected the financial model and with the revised output page in hand, Steven headed over to Ulrich's office to let him know what had happened.

———— • ————

It's unrealistic to think that mishaps, miscommunications, and outright screwups won't happen. They will. The goal, therefore, is damage control. When a mistake happens or a problem comes down the pipeline, the best thing to do is alert your teammates or supervisor early. Give your col-leagues ample warning and come armed with solutions before those initial mistakes or problems turn into some-thing bigger or worse.

This is called *raising a red flag,* and the goal is to highlight potential problems or pitfalls as early as possible and communicate your ability to fix them ASAP.

The Strategy

1. Highlight the issue.
2. State the rationale.
3. Propose a solution.

On-the-Job Case

1. Highlight the Issue

Ulrich, I hate to tell you this, but there's a mistake in the presentation we sent out to Hipster yesterday.

Transparency is key when things go wrong. People *always* prefer to know about problems sooner rather than later. Don't wait until something is beyond repair to let your team know. As soon as you spot a problem (or potential problem), let your team know immediately. No good will come of catching your manager off guard late in the game or surprising your colleagues at the last moment with bad news.

It can be tempting to try to sweep problems or screwups under the rug. It's not that hard to convince yourself that problems will disappear on their own if you just let them be. But that strategy is akin to playing Russian roulette with your career—you have absolutely no way of knowing, much less controlling, the outcome.

2.   State the Rationale

The output page must have grabbed cells from an outdated model and was therefore pasted in incorrectly.

The first two questions you'll likely hear when you make a mistake are "How did this happen?" and "Why did this happen?" You'll do far better if you're able to answer one or both of these questions up front. Think back to Chapter 2, "The Foolproof Download," and use the same template— lead with the punch line and state clearly the reason why or way in which something happened.

The goal is not to come up with an excuse, place blame, or skirt an issue. The goal is simply to lay out the facts and make your supervisor understand how or why something went wrong (or is about to go wrong) so that she'll have full information to act upon. Once you've given her a clear assessment of the situation, you can then move on to focus on the solution.

Information your boss might be looking for includes:

- Why is the project going to be late? What is the cause of the delay?
- What is wrong with the memo? Who provided bad/wrong/misleading information?
- How did the delivery manage to arrive at the wrong customer's address? Was it a purchasing error or a glitch in the inventory-control system?
- When will we have full information regarding the fund-raising campaign? What information is still outstanding?

- How did the newsletter go out with the wrong date? Who was responsible for editing/proofing and final quality control?

3. Propose a Solution

I've reviewed the entire presentation again and I'm absolutely certain everything is now correct. Would you like me to put in a call to the client to let them know, or should I just send the updated version and ask them to disregard yesterday's e-mail?

The question that most often follows "Why or how did that happen?" is "How can we fix it?" Having the ability to propose a good solution even in rocky situations can often be the difference between being a good employee and a great employee. If you do know how to solve your predicament, by all means go ahead and do so. Or share your proposed solution with your boss immediately and get his sign-off before making the fix.

If you don't have a solution in hand, try to offer a suggestion of possible courses of action. Throwing out a few good ideas or alternatives will likely help you and your boss get to the right answer quicker. Presenting your manager with several options goes a long way toward showing you as a thoughtful and proactive professional and problem solver.

———— • ————

Let's go back to Steven and Ulrich to see how Steven might have told Ulrich about the mistake in the client presentation.

1. HIGHLIGHT THE ISSUE

- I just realized there's an error in the presentation we sent to Hipster yesterday.
- Ulrich, I have some bad news about the Hipster presentation—I found an error in the output page as I was reviewing the slides.
- Unfortunately, as I was reviewing the slides this morning, I discovered an error on page thirty-two of the client presentation.
- Ulrich, I hate to tell you this, but there's a mistake in the presentation we sent out to Hipster yesterday.

2. STATE THE RATIONALE

- The cells didn't copy correctly. The output page must have grabbed cells from an outdated model.
- The client presentation doesn't have the latest numbers.
- One of the output pages was tied to a previous model that was out of date.
- I realized after reviewing the slides again that I made a mistake in one of the output pages. I've gone ahead and made the fix.

3. PROPOSE A SOLUTION

- I've checked all the numbers throughout the presentation again and corrected both the model and the presentation.
- I've reviewed the entire presentation again and I'm absolutely certain everything is now correct.
- Would you like me to put in a call to the client to let them know, or should I just send the updated version and ask them to disregard yesterday's e-mail?
- I'm happy to reach out to the client to let them know we'll be sending over a revised presentation this evening unless you think there's a better way to handle this.

Steven clearly and effectively told Ulrich up front about the problem (think "Foolproof Download" and leading with the punch line). He didn't make excuses or try to hide the facts. He was matter-of-fact and moved quickly on to the solution—he fixed the model and revised the output page.

Steven then proposed two alternative solutions, showing Ulrich that he had given the issue serious thought and didn't take the matter lightly. Should they put in a call to the client or just send the new presentation and politely ask the client to disregard the previous version?

In effect, Steven presented Ulrich not with a problem but with several options of how to solve a problem. He used transparency to highlight the problem, showed initiative in fixing the problem, and was generous in giving Ulrich various options to solve the issue.

The Apology

People get tripped up all the time by the apology. Should I apologize? How should I apologize? Does admitting blame make the situation worse? Do I look like a jerk if I don't apologize?

Apologies are complicated. As a general rule, you should use apologies when appropriate (i.e., when you screw up). The two key rules of a good apology are:

- Be sincere.
- Be succinct.

Being sincere means owning up to your mistakes—acknowledging the lapse in judgment, the less-than-stellar performance, or the missed results that got you into this mess in the first place—and then quickly moving on to how you are solving the problem.

Being succinct is critical because prolonging the apology keeps people focused on the negative, rather then encouraging and allowing them to move forward to the positive, the solution. Going on and on about how sorry you are doesn't do anyone any good.

Here is some good example language to use when you apologize.

THE APOLOGY

- I'm very sorry about the mistake in the memo, it won't happen again.
- I do apologize, I know we had a lot of versions of the model going back and forth, but it's my responsibility to make sure we're using the latest and greatest data.
- I hope you know that I feel badly about the mix-up and that I do apologize.
- I apologize for the mishandling of Adam's offer. We absolutely thought we were in the ballpark with his pay package.

Once you've apologized, move on. Don't dwell on the apology or give it more airtime than it deserves. You'll lose sight of what's truly important—fixing the issue and moving forward.

The Not-So-Quick Fix: Hadley Robinson, Human Resources Generalist

Hadley Robinson was an HR professional at a mid-size technology firm who worked in executive compensation and benefits. She had been working on a high-profile offer for a candidate for senior vice president. She and her team had done ample research before extending a final offer, but they hadn't done their homework well enough.

Upon receipt of the offer, Adam, the prospective candidate, threw a fit. Insulted with the pay package, Adam threatened to decline on the spot. Apparently, he was earning more at his current post. Something had gone very wrong, and Hadley and her team clearly lacked full information. It fell to Hadley to alert her boss, Micah, the director of HR, about the debacle. Hadley called Micah, asked for a few minutes of his time, then went down to his office to give him an update.

———— • ————

It would be unfair to say that in every instance you'll find the mistake, fix the financial model, paste in a new output page, and, presto, be home free. Life is often messier than that. Even when situations are less clear-cut, however, you can still follow the GOTJ action strategy, with a slight tweak to step 3, propose a solution.

When you don't have a clear-cut solution in mind, instead highlight that you're working on a solution and promise to keep your manager in the loop as you make progress.

The Strategy

1. Highlight the issue.
2. State the rationale.
3. Communicate next steps.

On-the-Job Case

Steps 1 and 2 are the same as in the first scenario.

3. Communicate Next Steps

We're doing everything we can to get our number in line with his expectation. I will come back to you as soon as I have more/better information. Is there anything else you'd like me to do in the meantime or do you have any other ideas?

If you can't propose a solution as in our earlier scenario (because you're not sure how to solve your problem), then focus instead on next steps and offer a plan of action that includes an idea of what to do, a promise to keep your manager in the loop as you make progress, and a request for input or feedback from him on your plan.

Here's some additional example language of what Hadley's conversation with Micah might have sounded like.

---

1. HIGHLIGHT THE ISSUE

- Micah, I need to fill you in on Adam's offer. He surprised our team by threatening to reject the offer and said he's making more in his current role.
- Micah, I want to post you on the status of Adam's offer. Unfortunately, there's been a disconnect between his expectations and our compensation calculation.
- I need to talk to you about Adam's offer. There's been a glitch and he's very unhappy with our offer.
- Micah, I have some bad news regarding Adam's offer. He's extremely unhappy with the pay package.

---

2. STATE THE RATIONALE

- Apparently, our number is lower than his current compensation and, he contends, not on par with his peers in the industry.
- We obviously didn't have full information when we calculated his compensation package.
- We thought we had a good sense of where his expectations would be, but it seems as though we were off base.
- Adam is arguing that we're at least twenty percent lower than his industry peers.

3. COMMUNICATE NEXT STEPS

- Our team is reworking the formula as we speak and getting additional information from Adam and from some of our colleagues at other firms.
- We're doing everything we can to get our number in line with his expectations.
- I will come back to you as soon as I have more/better information. Is there anything else you'd like me to do in the meantime?
- Do you have any recommendations of people to speak with as we work through this? Am I missing anything obvious here?

In this way, Hadley still approached her boss quickly with the information and laid out the situation clearly and concisely. Instead of having a quick fix, however, she let him know that she and the team were continuing to work on a solution. Hadley also brought Micah into the process— asking him if he had any ideas on how to proceed or thoughts of people to speak with as they tried to fix their problem.

———————— • ————————

How about time off? Have you ever needed to get away for an important family reunion, a wedding, or a community-service activity? How many times have you wondered how to handle an inconvenient but unavoidable absence?

Asking for time off is an issue that people struggle with all the time, especially if you're a banker or a lawyer and are expected to put in eighty-hour weeks. Or if you're an editorial assistant at *Vogue* working on the September issue, and you and your colleagues haven't had a weekend off since Memorial Day. How then are you going to get two full days away in the summer?

Do you just sneak out the door, cross your fingers, and hope no one notices? That's a pretty risky strategy. The better approach is to let your teams know early and make arrangements in advance to have your workload covered.

Anna Collins: *Mirabella* Magazine Summer Intern

Anna Collins was a summer intern at *Mirabella* who loved her job and coveted her access to high-fashion luminaries and designer bags. What she didn't love were the eighty-hour workweeks, but she told herself it was a minor price to pay for the chance to land her dream job.

Anna had a problem. Her best friend was getting married over July 4 weekend. That was smack in the middle of the production cycle for *Mirabella*'s September issue, and everyone knew that the September issue, with its fall-fashion preview, was the most important of the year in advertising dollars and pages. How was Anna going to disappear for two whole days?

Anna couldn't imagine missing the wedding, but she also couldn't imagine asking for the weekend off. Everyone worked weekends at *Mirabella*. Wouldn't it look bad if she was missing in action during the busiest time of the year? Would she ever get promoted to editorial assistant if she told her team she needed the weekend off? Should she just wait until the last minute, pray her team didn't need her, and slip out unannounced?

The Strategy—Asking for Time Off

1.   Highlight the issue.
2.   Cover your bases.
3.   Get buy-in.

As difficult as it sounds, it's always better to raise the issue early and remind your teams often. The strategy for asking for time off follows the same pattern of raising a red flag, but instead of simply stating a rationale and proposing a solution, you've got show how you've got your bases covered for your expected absence, then get the buy-in of your boss to green-light the weekend (or week or two) away.

Let your colleagues know well in advance, make arrangements to have your workload covered, and provide strategic reminders to ensure no one forgets at the last minute. The last thing you want is to have your senior editor looking for you while you're gone.

Susan, I'd like to talk to you about taking the weekend of July Fourth off. My closest friend is getting married in Maine. **[Highlight Issue]**

I wanted to let you know early so that we can plan accordingly. I will take care of everything I need to in advance, and I'll make sure that the team knows exactly where all of my pages stand. **[Cover Your Bases]**

Do you think that will be a problem or can we make it work? Is there anything else you'd like me to take care of in advance? **[Get Buy-in]**

1. HIGHLIGHT THE ISSUE

- Susan, I'd like to talk to you about taking the weekend of July Fourth off—my closest friend is getting married in Maine.
- Susan, I need to talk to you about taking several days off this summer.
- Susan, I'm hoping to be out of pocket on Saturday, July third, and Sunday, July Fourth, for an important wedding.

- James, I'm going to try not to be here on July third and the Fourth. I know we'll be coming up on the close for the September issue, but I've got a close friend's wedding in Chicago, and I'd like to do whatever it takes to make it there, even just for a short trip overnight.

2. COVER YOUR BASES

- I know it's not ideal to take time off in July, so I wanted to raise the issue early to see if we can make it work. I have a list of my deadlines and they will all be completed in advance.
- I wanted to let you know early enough so that we can plan accordingly and see who can help cover for me while I'm gone.
- I've spoken to Erica and she has agreed to cover for me for the weekend, assuming management is okay with it.
- I will of course take care of everything I need to in advance and be reachable by cell and e-mail the entire weekend if anything urgent comes up.

3. GET BUY-IN

- Does that sound doable? I know it's not ideal, but I'd really like to find a way to make it work.

- Do you think I can swing it? I'm willing to do whatever I need to do in advance to ensure that no one else will be affected by my absence.
- I can be back in the office Sunday evening if necessary, if that helps my cause.
- Is there anything else you'd like me to take care of in advance? I'm happy to sit down with you in the weeks leading up to it to make sure there are no last-minute surprises while I'm gone.

Like Steven, Hadley, and Anna, you'll do wonders for yourself if you're seen as the person who brings up issues in advance and who is able to resolve them on your own. By your being transparent and taking initiative, people will come to think of you as the "solution" person instead of the "problem" person. They will trust you and know that, even when things go wrong, you're going to tell it straight and do your best to right a wrong instead of trying to hide or cover up a problem.

TROUBLESHOOTING

Q: What if I don't have a solution to my problem? Should I still raise the issue?

A: In the worst-case scenario, when you really have no idea what direction to take, at the least let your manager know that you've thought about the problem and tried to come up with a solution. Show that you've put some time, energy, and thought into the situation. While you can't come up with a perfect plan of action, you do want to get credit for trying. Then you can engage your manager and ask for her guidance on how to proceed.

Here is some example language you can use.

- I've been thinking through all the different angles, but I'm still torn about what to do. I think there are two good options that may work.
- I've been racking my brain trying to come up with a solution that will work for everyone, but I'm coming up short. What do you think?
- Edward, I've been thinking about this all morning, and I'm just not sure what the right course of action is. I'd really like your input to help move this forward.
- Seth, we've been going around and around in circles with the marketing guys. Do you have a few minutes to step in and help think through this?

chapter nine

Manage a Crisis

Life is not a matter of holding good cards, but sometimes play-ing a poor hand well.

—CHINESE FORTUNE COOKIE

At times, raising a red flag simply won't work. You're past the point of being able to head off a potential problem. In that case, you have to switch to full-on crisis-management mode. It's hard to anticipate every roadblock or stumble. All the thoughtful planning and preparation in the world sometimes just isn't enough. When things do go wrong, it's your job to switch into damage-control mode and dem-onstrate your ability to right a wrong quickly and effec-tively.

Communicating through a crisis involves (1) taking ownership and accepting responsibility for a screwup; (2) figuring out how to fix a problem in the near term; and (3) committing to learn from your mistake to ensure the problem doesn't repeat itself.

While it's hard to anticipate, diagnose, and much less treat every type of crisis that will arise in business, this chapter will take a look at three of the most common types of screwups.

1. Missing a deadline
2. Missing the boat
3. Dropping the ball

Julie Brzeski, Event Planner

Julie Brzeski worked for an event-planning company in Breckenridge, Colorado, catering to the many corporate outings and destination weddings that sprouted up in town every summer and fall. Julie was working on a proposal for an outdoor mountaintop wedding for 125 guests and owed her boss a final proposal by Friday. The proposal was to include menu recommendations and budgets for three different scenarios—a plated sit-down dinner, a cocktail-party-style affair with carving stations and passed appetizers, and a Southwestern-themed buffet.

Julie went to work immediately on the event and quickly had a good sense of how the cocktail party and buffet would play out. The sit-down dinner was more complicated. Julie was having a hard time reaching her beef and trout vendor, and she was running out of time. By Thursday morning, Julie realized she wasn't going to be able to finish the proposal on time. With no word from her preferred vendor, Julie reached out to her boss the day before the deadline to let him know the proposal was going to be delayed.

Missing a Deadline

Missing a deadline is usually due to one of two things— either you don't have the resources available to complete a task, or you took more time than anticipated to finish the task, i.e., you ran out of time. (If you haven't even started, then skip to the "Dropping the Ball" section below).

Presumably, if you've been working on a project plan, a cost estimate, or an event schedule, you've completed some portion of the work before hitting your roadblock or running out of time.

The strategy for missing a deadline resembles the strategy used in Chapter 7, "Answer Questions (You Don't Know the Answers To)." Simply replace

1. Here's what I know
2. Here's what I don't know
3. Here's how I'll figure it out

with the following:

The Strategy

1. Here's what's been completed
2. Here's what's still outstanding
3. Here's how I'll finish the task

On-the-Job Case

1.   Here's What's Been Completed

Andres, I need to speak to you about the proposal for the 125-person wedding due tomorrow. I've got the buffet and cocktail-party options complete and ready to go to the client.

There's no rule that says you have to lead off with the bad news, and frankly, there's not a lot of good reason to do so. Assuming you have made progress on your assignment, there's no reason not to give yourself a plug and highlight the positive before quickly moving on the outstanding item or key issue.

This is not to say you should bury the lead. Going back to Chapter 2, "The Foolproof Download," you still want to get to the heart of the matter up front. Nonetheless, you can cushion the blow of the bad news and give it a positive spin by leading with the good news first. You are still being up front about the missed deadline, but you are also highlighting that real progress has been made, outstanding dinner option not withstanding.

So start with what has been completed—to show that you've haven't been sitting around eating bonbons or dreaming about your vacation to Mexico—before moving on to what still needs to be done.

2.   Here's What's Still Outstanding

Unfortunately, I'm still working through the plated-dinner option. I'm trying to arrange the best price for the client on the beef and trout entrées, but I haven't been able to confirm with our preferred vendor. I'm unfortunately going to need another day or two.

Be forthright about what is going to be delayed. Don't beat around the bush or try to hide behind an excuse. People always appreciate candor, especially when things are going badly. As long as you move quickly on to how you're finishing the task and moving the ball forward (read: fixing the problem), you should be able to recover using a combination of transparency and initiative.

3. Here's How I'll Finish the Task

I have several calls and e-mails in to our vendor, and I've reached out to some backup suppliers as well in case my guy doesn't pull through.

I have a couple of options for you: I can either get you the proposal and menus for the buffet and cocktail party to-morrow as planned and wait to get you the proposal for the plated dinner until next Monday; or I can hold off on the whole thing and give you one final document next Tuesday or Wednesday.

The only thing worse than hearing that a cost estimate or project proposal will be delayed is hearing that you don't know how long the delay will last or what it will cost. Coming up with a realistic revised plan of action and timing in advance is critical, and giving your delayed or revised timing is always a better consolation prize than having no backup plan at all. Have a proposed solution in hand when you walk into your manager's office or call your client on the phone.

Julie's update that gave Andres an idea of when she would come back with the plated-dinner pricing undoubtedly helped soften the blow of the initial delay. It gave Andres control over the process—at least he knew what was still outstanding, why the delay was taking place, and when he would hear back from Julie with a final proposal. It also gave him some control over next steps—did he want a half-baked proposal on time or a completed proposal several days late?

Here are some additional ways Julie might have told Andres about the delay:

1. HERE'S WHAT'S BEEN COMPLETED

- Andres, I want to give you an update on the Stanton wedding. I've got two of three scenarios complete and ready to go.
- Andres, I have an update for you on the wedding proposal for tomorrow. The cocktail-party and buffet options are ready for your sign-off.
- I want to fill you in on the wedding proposal for tomorrow; I'm in good shape on two of the three options for the client.
- Andres, I've got some great ideas about the cocktail party and the buffet for the Stanton wedding. I think you're really going to like where we came out.

2. HERE'S WHAT'S STILL OUTSTANDING

- Unfortunately, I'm still working through the plated-dinner option. I haven't heard back from my vendor on the beef and trout pricing.
- I'm not going to make the deadline tomorrow on the third piece. The plated dinner is turning out to be more complicated than I thought.
- I'm still working through the budget for the plated dinner, and I'm going to need a few more days to get back to you on final pricing.
- I hate to tell you, but I don't think I can realistically give you a final proposal on the third option until early next week. I still haven't confirmed pricing with my vendor.

3. HERE'S HOW I'LL FINISH THE TASK

- I need to check in with a few more suppliers regarding the buffalo beef and the trout before coming back with a final price.
- I can send you the proposal for the buffet and cocktail party tomorrow as planned but wait to get you the materials for the plated dinner until next Tuesday. Would that work?
- I'm doing my best to finish up as fast as I can, and I hope to have the final proposal to you by next Monday or Tuesday the latest.

- I will let you know as soon as I hear from my preferred supplier and/or I'd be happy to follow up with any other vendors you'd recommend.

Missing the Boat

Andrew Decker was a newly minted commercial real estate broker working with several veteran brokers while he learned the ropes his first month on the job. Andrew's first assignment was to prepare a report of all residential condo buildings in the Dallas area with more than one hundred apartments.

Andrew made sure he understood the parameters of the assignment before getting started. He spoke with several brokers to make sure the metrics he was looking at were the right ones—location, year built, school district, price per square foot, and common charges. He also planned to include qualitative information about the general condition of each building and the reputation of the management teams.

After spending several weeks compiling the data into a well-organized report, Andrew went to his boss, Hank, to present the information. Within minutes, Hank started peppering Andrew with questions and unraveling Andrew's analysis. How many buildings were full-service concierge or doorman buildings? Andrew didn't know. How many buildings had luxury amenities on-site, such as health clubs, pools, and spas? Again, Andrew didn't know. Hank then highlighted two buildings and dismissed them out of hand because they both had ground-floor commercial space, which would significantly impact common charges.

Hank told Andrew he needed to adjust for those three factors and rerun the data. Andrew explained that he had shown his data to several people and no one had mentioned taking into account whether the buildings were full service, offered certain amenities, or had ground-floor commercial space. Hank replied that people probably assumed Andrew would include those metrics as they were perhaps the most critical place to start for any residential analysis, especially in Dallas, where luxury properties were a dime a dozen.

Andrew maintained his composure and kept his disappointment to himself. Instead of letting Hank see his frustration (how could he have missed such an integral piece of the analysis?), Andrew replied thoughtfully with a matter-of-fact apology and a plan to revise the analysis and move forward.

The Strategy

1. Explain your approach.
2. Acknowledge feedback.
3. Offer revised action plan.

On-the-Job Case

1. Explain Your Approach

Hank, I understand your comments and I apologize for not including the metrics you just mentioned. I did reach out to

several brokers to get their sign-off on my approach, but I sup-
pose I was too narrowly focused on the basics.

When you screw up, it's helpful to give your manager a window into your thought process so he understands how or why you did something. Many times, people go down the wrong path even when they thought they had a valid reason for their actions.

Andrew thought he was doing a thorough job reaching out to other brokers to confirm he was looking at the right metrics for his analysis. Sharing his approach and rationale at least gave Hank an idea of Andrew's good intentions and strong work ethic. Andrew wasn't just being lazy or trying to get the report done quickly, he sincerely thought he had a done a good job on the assignment.

Moreover, opening up about why or how you did something creates an opportunity for a teachable moment. Hank then had an opportunity to respond and show Andrew why or how his analysis was wrong and how to fix it.

2. Acknowledge Feedback

Clearly, I wasn't thinking about the luxury amenities, but I
appreciate that those parameters are important to clients and
play a big role in valuing a residential property.

When you fail to meet expectations, it's important to understand how and why and then come up with a plan to meet or exceed them going forward.

Hank pointed out exactly what Andrew's analysis was missing and gave him clear guidance about how to fix the problem. Andrew had a good outline of how to move forward. You won't always be as lucky. If you're not given the information you need to move in the right direction, you need to go ahead and ask for it. The next section will give you some ideas of pointed questions you can ask to get the guidance you need to correct your work product or reverse course.

3. Offer Revised Action Plan

I can give you a revised analysis with both sets of data by early next week. Does that timing work for you? Is there anything else you'd like me to think about or include this time around that we haven't discussed?

As always, the most important step is how you're going to fix the analysis—what will you do and when will you have it by? Lay out your action plan and get the buy-in of your boss to avoid a second round of missed expectations or deadlines.

The following example language should serve as a helpful guide when you miss the boat on a task.

1. YOUR APPROACH

- Hank, I understand your comments and I apologize for not including the metrics you just mentioned.
- I reached out to several brokers to get their sign-off on my approach, but I suppose I was too narrowly focused on the basics.

- I assumed that location and price per square foot were the most important, but I clearly have a lot to learn.
- That makes a lot of sense. I focused on the basics but I can see how luxury properties differ from the rest of the market.

2. ACKNOWLEDGE FEEDBACK

- Hearing you mention these features now certainly makes sense, and I can see how those amenities are on par with location, price per square foot, and school district.
- Clearly, I wasn't thinking about the luxury amenities, but I appreciate that those parameters are important and play a big role in valuing a residential property.
- Hank, I appreciate your comments and completely agree. Now that you mention it, I can certainly see why ground-floor commercial space and luxury amenities are vital to the analysis.
- I appreciate your feedback. This has been a good learning experience for me, and I'll be sure to include these parameters going forward.

3. REVISED ACTION PLAN

- Let me revisit the analysis and come back to you in the next few days with another cut at the data.
- I'll go ahead and separate out the ground-floor commercial properties first and then rerun the analysis to include the luxury amenities and full-service buildings.
- I can give you a revised analysis with both sets of data by early next week. Does that timing work for you?
- Is there anything else you'd like me to think about or include this time around that we haven't talked about?

You won't always get the feedback and direction you need to take your task over the finish line or do something well that you've previously done poorly. Had Hank not laid out the exact steps Andrew needed to fix his anlysis, Andrew would have had to ask for feedback to fix, correct, improve, or complete the assignment. Here's some example language Andrew could have used to ask for this feedback.

ASK FOR FEEDBACK

- How can I improve upon the analysis so it meets your needs? What else should I be including or excluding in a second draft?

- Can we talk a little bit about what's missing from the analysis so I can make the necessary adjustments?
- What should I be doing differently to make the analysis more relevant?
- Is there anything else to think about before I take another crack at this?

Dropping the Ball

It's not often that you forget to do something entirely or reach a deadline without even starting on an assignment. But it happens to the best of us. Someone reading this book right now has completely blown through a deadline or just plumb forgotten to do something on his or her to-do list.

Cleaning up the mess after totally dropping the ball is actually pretty simple—mostly because there's not much you can do other than apologize and offer to get to the task ASAP. To the extent that you have a good reason for the delay (not many of us do), by all means share it. Otherwise, this strategy is pretty quick and to the point.

The Strategy

1. Apologize.
2. State your rationale.
3. Promise to do it ASAP.

On-the-Job Case

1.   Apologize

Brian, the memo has been on my radar all month and I apologize, I haven't had a chance to get to it yet.

In the case of totally dropping the ball and completely forgetting to do something, there's not much you can do other than apologize. Take ownership for the mess-up and admit that you made an error—either in judgment or timing or planning.

2.   State Your Rationale

I've been juggling a hundred and one things this week and I must have just forgotten to put in the call.

People use a variety of reasons or excuses in this situation— some of which are valid and others which are not and should be avoided. A valid excuse might be that you've been tied up on another, arguably more important project and you simply haven't had a moment to lift your head up from your desk to get to anything else.

Beyond being totally absorbed in more important tasks, everything else starts to fall in the not-so-valid category. See below for some language to employ when you simply forgot, misjudged your time, or blew through a deadline entirely.

3. Promise to Do It ASAP

Let me put it on the top of my list and spend the next twenty-four hours focused on the report. I promise to have something for you by the end of the day tomorrow.

Once you've forgotten to do something, assume unless otherwise directed that this task now moves to the top of your list. Give it urgent priority so that you can quickly clear up the matter. It never shows well to miss something completely and then promise to get to it next week or in a couple of days. No matter how busy you are, stop what you are doing and take care of this matter urgently.

Here is some example language that you can follow when you've completely dropped the ball on a task.

---

1. APOLOGIZE

- Evan, I am so sorry. I don't know how I missed that.
- Schade, I feel awful. It was on my list and somehow it must have just slipped through the cracks. I'm very sorry.
- Brian, the memo has been on my radar all month and I apologize. I haven't had a chance to get to it yet.
- Navya, I know I owe you a proposal by this afternoon, but I apologize, I'm not going to have it in time.

---

2. STATE THE RATIONALE

- I've been juggling a hundred and one things this week and I must have just forgotten to put in the call.
- I've been tied up all day on putting together a presentation for Robert and I haven't had a chance to take a breath, much less focus on your memo.
- I am completely consumed with the president's speech for next week's annual event, and I'm not going to have a chance to get to it until tomorrow.
- I wish I had a good excuse for you, but it just completely fell off my radar.

3. GET TO IT ASAP

- I will go reach out to the marketing team right now and come back to you as soon as I put the materials together.
- Let me put it on the top of my list and spend the next twenty-four hours focused on the report. I promise to have something for you by the end of the day tomorrow.
- I've moved it to the top of my list and I will get started right away.
- I will clear my calendar for the rest of the day and get to it this afternoon. I should be able to get you a first draft this evening.

TROUBLESHOOTING

Q: What if I don't think I missed the boat? I felt that my work was spot-on?

A: You are entitled to respectfully disagree with your boss if you think a deliverable or assignment is well-done. If you want to push back on your manager and stand your ground, then do so in a nonconfrontational and objective way. Do this by focusing on the assignment instead of on the "he says / she says" of who is right or wrong.

For instance, if you think the recommendations in the annual report are right or you think the press release absolutely hits the key selling points your client is looking for, then provide the rationale behind this thinking. Just as in chapter 6, "Ask for Feedback," you want to be able to point to some anecdotal evidence or other type of "proof" to argue your case.

Here is the strategy to make your case effectively and politely.

1. Acknowledge alternative opinion/position.
2. Respectfully disagree.
3. State your position.

Here is some example language you can use.

1. ACKNOWLEDGE ALTERNATIVE OPINION/POSITION

- Charlie, I hear what you're saying.
- Michael, I understand your position.
- Noah, I appreciate where you're coming from.
- Stanley, your point is well-taken.

2. RESPECTFULLY DISAGREE

- However, I respectfully disagree.
- Unfortunately, I'm coming out on this with a different opinion than you are.
- Nonetheless, I still think the right approach is . . .
- Your comments notwithstanding, I still think we're coming at this from different angles.

3. STATE YOUR POSITION

- I think the key selling points should reflect the new product launch and expansion to China.
- My preference is to increase the advertising budget by twenty percent.
- I think the metrics I used are the right ones for the analysis.
- I'd argue in favor of waiting for the new product rollout before making any big decisions on advertising.

part four

---

sell yourself

chapter ten

Your Personal Elevator Pitch

Your personal pitch is essentially the bait that you are fishing with, and the key question to ask yourself is this: What are you trying to catch?

—Michael Corddry, Founder, Lansing Capital

Have you ever been seated next to your boss's boss at the annual company barbecue? Are you the lucky (or unlucky, depending on your vantage point) soul who finds yourself riding up the elevator with the president of your firm? If that's you, do you find yourself staring intently at your BlackBerry, hoping she doesn't notice you? Or, are you one of the rarefied few, a brave soul who introduces yourself, impresses the bigwig with your poise and articulate introduction of yourself, and leaves her thinking, *Wow, he's someone to watch out for!* Not many of us out there are able to pull off the personal elevator pitch (yes, it really happens) in a meaningful and impactful way.

Out of fear or mere complacency, most of us choose to bury ourselves in the comfort of our smartphone or BlackBerry and hope that the boss's boss will excuse herself before we have to engage in a serious discussion. After all, what could we possibly say that would sound interesting, smart, or novel? We're so sure we'll sound like a boob that we keep our mouths shut and prefer making no impression at all to making a bad one. Of course, you kick yourself afterward thinking about the missed opportunity, but comfort yourself thinking that you would probably have screwed it up anyway.

———— • ————

Crafting a personal elevator pitch is one of the more difficult things to do in business. Entrepreneurs spend much time thinking about their elevator pitch when they're trying to raise capital or get people excited about their new business. New grads and career switchers think long and hard about their personal pitch when they're looking for a new job or interviewing with an employer.

But entrepreneurs looking to raise capital and newly minted grads looking for a job aren't the only ones selling themselves regularly. You are too. As a professional, you are continually presenting and promoting (read: marketing) yourself to others.

Once you've landed that great new job or hard-won promotion, it's arguably more important than ever to be able to articulate who you are, what you do, and how you're unique. Or, once that great new job or hard-won promotion turns into a humdrum job with no career advancement in sight, you've got to think yet again about leveraging your network and plotting your next move. With each new introduction to colleagues, clients, or senior management, you want to make a positive first impression. Who knows where the relationship may lead?

———— • ————

Brian Walls, a senior executive at a manufacturing firm, once told me about a great young hire named Rebecca who made a name for herself in the office at lightning speed. Brian received no less than five different calls from directors and vice presidents within Rebecca's first month on the job, telling him to look out for the rising young star.

Every single one of those senior managers met Rebecca at a company networking or social event. In every case, she extended her hand, introduced herself, and made such a positive impression that the buzz around the office was fast and furious—they could tell she'd be a success.

One has to wonder what Rebecca could possibly have said or done to leave such an indelible mark. While I don't know what, specifically, she said or did, I do know she didn't stand around staring at her BlackBerry, avoiding people. I know that Rebecca took the initiative to engage her senior colleagues, thought about her story in advance, and no doubt prepared for and practiced how to introduce herself. How do I know that?

Rebecca could not possibly have made the impression she did had she not spent time thinking in advance about who she was, why she joined the firm, what she hoped to do in the future, and how her previous experiences tied into or uniquely qualified her for her current role.

What about charisma? you might say. Or charm? Or just a natural gift for gab? Maybe she had it. Rebecca probably had a healthy dose of poise and confidence to boot, but that's certainly not all. No matter how engaging or charismatic you may be, you'll go only so far without a compelling or engaging personal story to go along with it.

So there goes Rebecca, making a good impression, not to get a new job or a promotion, but simply to blaze a trail within her new organization. Rebecca recognized that approaching her colleagues and engaging with senior leadership was a good way to start off on the right foot and get noticed within her organization quickly.

Different Person, Different Pitch

A famous attorney once said that his gift was being able to decide, of all the potential stories to tell a jury, which one would resonate the most. That is your job with the personal elevator pitch as well—deciding which story will resonate with your particular audience. Running into your boss's boss is different from running into a family friend. Meeting a senior executive for the first time is different from meeting a potential new client.

Just as you probably have multiple online profiles—Facebook, LinkedIn, Twitter—you should also understand that different situations warrant different pitches or stories. What parts of your background (academic, personal, professional) do you want to highlight? What experiences have been most influential or transformative for you?

Understanding the different elements of your story and being able to use those elements effectively depending on the audience and your objectives will enable you to position yourself effectively no matter the situation.

Typically, a good personal pitch has two primary

goals—you're either looking to make a good impression or to enhance your professional network. The two can be complementary, but each serves its own purpose. Here's how I define each.

Make a Good Impression

- Sound übersmart and impressive—either know your functional area cold or be well-informed and opinionated about life outside your functional area—either can work depending on the situation.
- Make someone want to work with you or for you.
- Make someone want you to work for them and/or advocate for you—put you on a fast track, promote or compensate you well.
- Show how good you are at what you do without coming across as pompous.

Enhance Your Professional Network

- Increase the number of people you know.
- Improve the quality of people who consider you a friend, resource, colleague, client (i.e., is your network composed of up-and-comers, decision makers, influencers, well-connected professionals?).

Once you think about your objectives, you can begin to think about crafting your story.

———— • ————

This chapter will highlight several different people's personal pitches in various situations, all with their own spin on their story, and all with their own motive—are they trying to impress the boss or convince a new colleague they're the right person for the job? Are they transitioning to a new job or hoping to move up the ranks from the one they already have? No matter the scenario, they all follow the Great on the Job strategy.

The Strategy

1. The punch line / destination
2. The backstory
3. Connect the dots / forward momentum

On-the-Job Case

1. The Punch Line

As discussed in Chapter 2, "The Foolproof Download," the punch line is the key concept you're trying to get across. Who are you? Why are you interesting, important, different? What is the key message you want people to take away about you? Rather than leave it for the end, your punch line, the key piece of information that you want to share about yourself, should come front and center.

What is your agenda or goal? Are you trying to look smart in front of new colleagues at a company function or just trying to impress the boss? Is the goal to meet new people at an industry event or network so you can make a career jump? With each new introduction, are you trying to improve the quality of your professional network by meeting movers and shakers, or just come across as smart and confident?

Everyone has different bait, and everyone has a different agenda. Sometimes that bait and agenda change based on the environment—your personal pitch might sound very different when you're talking to the boss rather than a family friend. You might use one version of your story at an internal work event, trying to make a good impression, and another at a networking or industry event, trying to enhance your professional network.

If you're a job seeker or a career switcher, the punch line is easy—it's your destination: What do you want to be when you grow up? If you're not looking for a new job, here are a few questions to prompt your thinking about your punch line.

Think Relevant, Not Recent

People often think and talk about themselves in reverse chronological order, even when their most recent experiences aren't the most relevant. No rule says you have to start with your bio and go backward through your life.

If you're a computer programmer who's been investing money on the side for five years and then decides to go back to school to learn about investment management, the relevant part of your story is that you've been managing your money for the past five years, not that you've worked in computer programming.

Don't be afraid to focus on the relevant aspects of your story even if they're not the most recent or most central in how you've been spending your time or earning your keep. Relevant information trumps recent information every time. A money manager wants to hear about your personal returns rather than your responsibilities coding software.

Why are you great at what you do?

What is the reason why or way in which you're a star? For example, I'm a media trainer and consultant. As a former producer on *Oprah,* I know what TV producers are looking for, and I can always come up with the compelling hook to sell your story. Or, I started my own PR firm after spending ten years in journalism. I had been pitched enough stories to know what a good news hook is. Or, I'm a great salesman. I connect with people and understand what they want. You give me a product I believe in and I can sell the hell out of it.

Why do you love what you do?

I'm passionate about saving our planet and creating great products along the way, so I'm committed to Patagonia's product-development group. Or, I'm a fantastic divorce attorney because I'm hypercommitted to my clients and I'm intellectually challenged by each new case.

How do you differentiate yourself?

What is your competitive advantage? What sets you apart from the pack? You might say: I run the most popular women's clothing boutique in Nashville because I will do anything and everything for my customers, and I offer loyalty discounts that are unmatched.

How or why are you unique or memorable?

Is it because of the path you took to get you where you are or the road ahead you're looking to go down? I recently met a college sophomore from Las Vegas at the Cornell School of Hotel Administration. His dream is to bring the first "green" casino to the Strip. He knows and loves the hospitality industry, and he's intrigued by alternative energy. He's combined the two to create an ambitious goal for himself and a personal story that recruiters won't hear from anyone else.

You need to be able to answer one or more of these questions yourself so that you can communicate your story or value to others at the moment of truth—when you run into a colleague casually at work, the boss at a social gathering, or a potential client on the ninth hole.

2.   The Backstory

How did you get here? What did you do before? What was your motivation or rationale for getting to the point you are at now?

Have you always had a passion for food and known you wanted to be a nutritionist from a young age? Did you have a transformative experience in college or traveling throughout South America that made you realize you wanted to be a health-care emergency worker? Have you spent the last fifteen years honing your skills so you know the insurance business cold? Did you grow up playing poker, watching the ticker tape, and then find Wall Street was a logical place to land after college?

Or, if you simply fell into your job or role, what is the story you tell people so it comes across as interesting and intentional? (No one is impressed with the guy who says he's an accountant because he couldn't think of anything else to do with his life.) How do you make sense of your story in a compelling way to communicate that you're doing what you're meant to do?

3.   Connect the Dots / Forward Momentum

Years ago as I interviewed for a position on Wall Street, a senior banker asked how I would handle the grueling work schedule and the hundred-hour weeks. I replied that as a Peace Corps volunteer, I was effectively on duty for two years straight. I was the only Peace Corps volunteer in my town, and the only American living within a fifty-mile radius. As a representative of the United States, I was considered an ambassador of my country. My every move, both personal and professional, was watched and scrutinized by my tiny town of twelve hundred people. I didn't have the luxury of turning off work while I was abroad.

So, I explained that I was working 168 hours a week. The interviewer gave a nod of approval and we moved on. When I got an offer the following week, he told me how impressed he was with that answer. Although it was a stretch, the story resonated and connected two disparate experiences for me and the interviewer.

Similarly, when I introduced myself to new colleagues at Exxon Mobil and they asked what I did before business school, you can imagine the challenge I had in explaining that I was a policy analyst at the Environmental Protection Agency. Nonetheless, I had given the move a lot of thought beforehand and was able to answer people's objections before they even voiced them.

"I'm here because I'm interested in global energy policy. I don't think it's fair to only look at the issue from one side. I want to see how a big energy company operates so that I have a balanced and informed opinion." I would add with a smile, "I do also happen to drive a car and use electricity."

How or why does it all make sense? How do you tie together your varied and disparate experiences? How do you connect for people the dots of what you've done in the past with what you're doing now and what you hope to be doing in the future?

Or, if you're with a company or new to an organization, what are you excited about going forward? How do you show that you're an achiever, a rising star? What new projects are you working on or new ideas do you bring to the table? Giving people an idea of what your future looks like is a great way to get them engaged in your professional development.

———— • ————

As we go through the remainder of the chapter, we'll take a look at four different scenarios of young professionals who use their personal elevator pitches in different ways in different environments. Avery, an ad sales rep, is trying to impress her boss. Jonathan, a career switcher, is trying to prove himself to his new colleagues. Avery, the same sales rep, now finds herself with an old colleague who may help her return to her previous profession. And finally, Kate is looking to make a career switch and put together the pieces of her interviewing pitch.

1. **The Impresser (Avery):** the employee trying to impress her boss during a casual run-in.

2. **The Convincer (Jonathan):** the recent career switcher who must introduce himself to his new colleagues in a compelling way.

3. **The Opportunist (Avery):** the unfulfilled professional looking for a new career opportunity.

4. **The Natural (Kate):** the career switcher or the "I know I look like a chemist but I really belong in corporate finance."

1. The Impresser:
The Run-in with the Boss

The scenario: You are seated next to the boss at the company barbecue

The goal: To impress her with the great job you're doing in your position

Avery Richards was an account manager for Pembroke Media, a midsize advertising publisher in Chicago. Avery sold advertising pages to private schools, educational institutions, and summer camps for publication in cultural magazines, such as the Kohl's Children's Museum guide, the Chicago Botanic Garden magazine, and the Ravinia Music Festival guide.

The president of the company, Margaret Bai, hosted a summer outing every year for Pembroke staff and spouses. Outside of that event, Avery had little opportunity to interact with Margaret. Avery reported directly to the VP of sales and had probably had a total of three conversations with Margaret in the previous year.

Avery was determined not to let this opportunity go to waste. She had just closed her best quarter yet, and the client relationships she had been nurturing for the past twelve months were finally starting to materialize. Her background as an elementary-school teacher had put her in a great position with all of her private-school clients—she knew many of the administrators, and as a former teacher, she was great at relating to admission directors and understanding their motivation behind advertising and promotions.

As Avery mingled with everyone, she spotted Margaret out of the corner of her eye. Now or never, she thought, as she approached Margaret.

The Strategy

1. The punch line: Most important/relevant recent accomplishment
2. The backstory: What brought you to this position?
3. Forward momentum: What are you excited about going forward?

Avery: Hi, Margaret, how are you? Thanks so much for having us again this year. It's so nice to see everyone outside of the office.

Margaret: I'm glad you could make it, Avery. How are things going?

Avery: Things are great, thanks for asking. I'm thrilled to have just had my best quarter yet with thirty pages in the Kohl's summer guide. I'm really building some leverage into my client relationships—each sale gets a little easier these days, and new-business lead times are getting shorter. **[Punch Line]**

Margaret: That's great news, I'm glad to hear it.

Avery: You know, I think the schools really appreciate that as a former teacher I can relate to their challenges. **[Backstory]**

Margaret: Absolutely. It's certainly one of your competitive advantages for sure.

Avery: And I don't know if Michael had a chance to mention it or not yet but I've been thinking about creating a "Summer Fun" page to bring in some of my target accounts that aren't ready to jump in with a full-page ad. I think dividing up the page into ten mini-sections with like-minded accounts may be an interesting way to go, so I'm starting to feel out a few potential target accounts. **[Forward Momentum]**

Margaret: Good for you. Michael did mention something briefly, but I wasn't clear about the details so it's great to hear it from the source. One thing you may want to consider . . .

Avery: Thanks, that a great suggestion. And how about you, how is everything going on your end?

Here is some additional example language Avery could have used in her conversation with Margaret.

1. PUNCH LINE

- I'm great, thanks! I'm proud to have just closed a great quarter with thirty pages in the summer Kohl's guide.
- I've just had my best quarter yet with thirty pages in the Kohl's Children's guide.
- Things are going great—I'm really starting to build momentum into my client relationships, and the lead times for winning new accounts are getting shorter.
- I'm doing really well—this quarter has been a huge success for me.

2. THE BACKSTORY

- You know, I think my clients really appreciate that I'm a former teacher.
- It's easy for me to relate to my clients. I understand what drives their buying decisions.
- I'm really able to empathize with admissions directors who are losing families due to the current economic environment.
- I knew the switch from teaching to sales would be difficult, but it turns out that my background has been a huge asset actually.

---

3. FORWARD MOMENTUM

- I'm thinking about how to draw in new clients and I'm considering a "Summer Fun" page to sell mini-ads to new schools or summer camps.
- With five schools and five camps, it would be a great page to be part of for the new accounts and good business development for us.
- I've been toying around with a new idea to bring in first-time accounts.
- I've been hoping to talk to you about an idea I'm working on to bring in new accounts with mini-ads in a "Summer Fun" type page.

Even if Avery hadn't had the foresight to approach Margaret at the barbecue, Avery should have had these talking points ready so that if a run-in did happen, she would be ready to engage Margaret in a thoughtful dialogue and to impress her with her recent accomplishments and upcoming endeavors.

2. The Convincer: What Did You Say You Did Again Before Joining the Company?

The scenario: You've just made a career switch

The goal: To introduce yourself to new colleagues and show that you're perfectly suited to your new challenge

Jonathan Lindgren always knew he wanted to be an architect. However, three years into his career at a small firm, Jonathan realized he had made a huge mistake. He was no longer passionate about his work, and he didn't like the long life cycle of his product. Jonathan hated that in two years he hadn't seen a single building break ground, much less get built.

Jonathan decided to make a change. He began reaching out to friends and family to think about alternative career paths. Some friends in marketing urged him to consider the consumer products industry. Jonathan had never worked in a corporate environment and didn't know a thing about marketing or strategy. He had been sitting in front of an oversize table drafting plans for three years, calculating dimensions and ratios and studying angles and floor plans.

Little by little, however, Jonathan became excited about the prospect of going to work for corporate America, though his excitement was mixed with trepidation. What could an architect pretend to know about convincing men to drink Gatorade or women to buy running shoes?

Jonathan thought about the qualities that drew him to architecture in the first place and the skills he possessed that were transferable. He was great with details and process-oriented thinking. He was accustomed to delving into his clients' business operations and easily navigating between big ideas and small details. He realized that brand management wasn't as far-fetched as he originally thought. It actually provided a logical and natural application of capabilities he had developed as an architect.

Jonathan applied this connective thinking to his story while interviewing for marketing jobs, and he used the

Think Skills-Based Versus Industry- or Experience-Based

What skills do you have that are transferable? Are you a big-picture thinker or more comfortable in the weeds?

Are you a great listener or writer or a skilled public speaker?

Forget industry-based or experienced-based skills and think about what you're good at naturally, then figure out how to apply that skill set to the job you're looking for.

same language when introducing himself to his new colleagues at McNell, who looked at him quizzically his first week on the job. After he highlighted his problem-solving and skills-based qualifications to justify his career switch, people dismissed their initial bias of "You're an architect turned brand manager?" and switched to "Great to have you on the team, we're looking forward to your perspective on our new product launch."

Let's take a look at what Jonathan's elevator pitch might have sounded like during his first week at McNell, as he introduced himself to his new colleagues.

The Strategy

1. The punch line: Who you are?
2. The backstory: What brings you to McNell?
3. Connect the dots: Why does this career switch make sense?

Jonathan: Hi, Stuart, do you have a moment? I'm Jonathan Lindgren and I just wanted to stop by and introduce myself. I just started here on the Splenda account in the Nutritionals Group. **[Punch Line]**

Stuart: Hi, Jonathan, welcome aboard. Thanks for stopping by.

Jonathan: My pleasure.

Stuart: What were you doing before joining McNell?

Jonathan: I have a pretty unique background, actually. I studied architecture in college and worked for a design firm for three years before making the switch to consumer products. **[Backstory]**

Stuart: Well, that's not a career path you hear every day. I don't think I've ever worked with a former architect before.

Jonathan: I know, I've been getting that a lot this week. The truth is, I've always been intrigued by what drives consumer habits, and I'm a data-driven person by nature. I wanted to be able to contribute to projects where I could see the beginning, middle, and end within a reasonable time frame, which doesn't happen too often with hundred-story buildings. **[Backstory]**

Stuart: That's an interesting analogy. I wouldn't have thought of that.

Jonathan: Yep, it turns out that architecture and brand management, at least in my mind, have a lot in common—you have to really be able to navigate between big ideas and small details, and that appealed to me. **[Connect the Dots]**

Stuart: Well, thanks so much for stopping by, I appreciate it. Good luck and please let me know if you need anything.

Jonathan: Thanks so much, I will certainly do that. I'm sure I'll have some questions for you in the next few weeks. It was a pleasure meeting you.

Here is some additional example language Jonathan could have used with his new colleagues.

1. PUNCH LINE
• I just joined the Nutritionals Group and I'll be working on the Splenda team. • I'm new to brand management and I'm happy to be part of the team. • I just made the jump from architecture to brand management, which I'm sure isn't something you hear every day. • I'm new to the organization, I actually just joined the Splenda team.

2. THE BACKSTORY

- I have a pretty unique background, actually. I studied architecture in college and worked for a design firm for three years.
- I've always been intrigued by what drives consumer habits, and I'm a data-driven person by nature.
- I love project work and I wanted to contribute to projects where I could see the beginning, middle, and end within a reasonable time frame.
- I jumped to consumer products after three long years working as an architect.

3. CONNECT THE DOTS

- The attention to detail and ability to take big ideas and convert them into tangible projects really appeals to me and attracted me to the industry.
- I think architecture and brand management have a lot in common—you have to be able to navigate between big ideas and small details.
- As I decided to consider new career options, I became intrigued with brand management.
- I actually think my skill set is well aligned with what it takes to succeed around here—an attention to detail and a client-driven mind-set.

He anticipated the "Why brand management?" questions his career change was sure to prompt. By connecting architecture and brand management in a way that made sense (big ideas, small details), he was able to position himself in a positive light. He effectively shifted the conversation from "He's unqualified and I don't want to work with him" to "He's smart and has new ideas to bring to the table."

3. The Opportunist: The Unfulfilled Professional Looking for a New Career Opportunity

The scenario: You are looking to make a job switch

The goal: To make someone take a chance on you

Avery from Pembroke Media left one key piece of information out from her conversation with her boss, Margaret, at the company picnic. While Avery had just had her best quarter yet, teaching in suburban Chicago still paid better than her part-time job selling advertising. If the opportunity arose, Avery would consider making the jump back to teaching.

One afternoon, Avery ran into Denise, the principal of a public elementary school in her district whom she had known for years. Avery realized immediately that this chance encounter was a great opportunity to reconnect with someone influential in her field. The best thing

Avery had going for her at that moment was that she had envisioned this scenario many times and gone through in her head what the dialogue would sound like.

As they exchanged pleasantries, Avery launched in to her personal pitch to express her interest in going back to teaching and explain away her four-year sabbatical.

The Strategy

1. The punch line: Your destination
2. The backstory: What you've been doing
3. Forward momentum: Next steps

The Hello and Good-Bye Make a Comeback

Don't forget to always bookend your elevator pitch with a hello and a good-bye. "Do you have a moment?" serves as the appropriate opener when you're dropping by someone's office to introduce yourself.

And the thanks (for your help or your time) comes with the forward momentum—how will you stay in touch, follow up, ask for help, or return the favor? Be sure to keep that proverbial door open after meeting new people around the office.

Avery quickly let Denise know she was looking to go back to teaching even though she had left the profession four years earlier. She then went into her backstory— talking about why she had left teaching (she had a baby), what she had done in the meantime (tutoring and advertising sales part-time)—then asked Denise for her thoughts on people to speak with or actions to take to start making the transition back to teaching. Let's take a look at what their conversation might have sounded like.

Avery: Hi, Denise, how are you? It's so great to see you!

Denise: Avery, hello, so nice to see you too! How are you?

Avery: I'm great, thanks.

Denise: Where are you teaching these days? I haven't seen you in ages.

Avery: Actually, I'm looking for a new position. I left Chicago City Day in 2007, but I've been thinking a lot lately about going back to teaching. I'm just starting to reach out to friends and colleagues to see how to make that happen. **[Destination]**

Denise: I had no idea you'd left Chicago City Day. I'm so surprised to hear that, you were always one of the best.

Avery: Oh, you're so kind, thanks. I had a baby and wanted to be home with him, so I've been tutoring and working for a small advertising publisher part-time managing their education accounts. Flexibility was really important to me, and the break allowed me to stay involved in the field without staying on board full-time. **[Backstory]**

Denise: I completely understand, it's always a challenge. I'm sure City Day was sad to see you go.

Avery: It was really hard for me too. I've missed teaching so much, but I'm ready now to come back on board. I'd love to pick your brain about any thoughts you have or people you might recommend I get in touch with. Would it be okay to follow up with you and set up a quick call or a meeting? **[Forward Momentum]**

Denise: Absolutely. Why don't you shoot me an e-mail and we can go grab coffee next month. I'll put my thinking cap on as well and see what we've got available in the district.

Avery: That would be fantastic, thank you so much, I really appreciate it! I'll shoot you an e-mail this week to follow up. Have a great week!

Here's some more example language of what Avery might have said to Denise.

---

1. DESTINATION

- Actually, I'm looking for a new position. I left Chicago City Day in 2007, but I've been thinking a lot lately about going back to teaching.
- Denise, what a treat to run into you! If you can believe it, I'm in the market for a new teaching position.
- I'm looking for a new job as a matter of fact, ideally teaching K–3 in the suburbs.

- I'm actually trying to go back to teaching—I wound up leaving in 2007 after having a baby, but I've missed it so much and I know it's what I'm meant to do.

2. THE BACKSTORY

- I've been working part-time as a reading and math tutor for the last few years.
- I work for a small advertising publisher managing their educational accounts, which is great; it's kept me connected to the field.
- I actually left teaching in 2007 after having a baby—I wanted to be home with him for the first few years.
- I've been thinking a lot about going back to teaching full-time. I really miss it.

3. FORWARD MOMENTUM

- I'd love to pick your brain about any thoughts you have or people you might recommend I get in touch with. Would it be okay to follow up with you and set up a quick call or a meeting?
- It's so nice to run into you today. As I begin to think about returning to teaching, I was actually going to reach out to you.

- Do you have any recommendations of people I could speak with? You must know anyone and everyone in the district.
- Would you like to grab coffee one day? I'd love talk with you at some point if you have the time.

Avery led off immediately with her intended goal of going back to teaching, then emphasized to Denise that she'd stayed involved in education while on sabbatical by highlighting her part-time tutoring and educational-account client base.

It's also worth noting that Avery's elevator pitch to Margaret, her boss, was completely different from her pitch to Denise, the principal. They drew on different pieces of Avery's experiences and background and were crafted with different goals and objectives in mind. The first was aimed at making a good impression on her current boss; the second was crafted to help launch a career transition.

The goal for everyone is to know which pieces of their story resonate with which audience, then to be able to pull those relevant pieces in at the right time.

4. The Natural: "I Know I Look Like a Chemist but I Really Should Be Working in Corporate Finance."

The scenario: You are looking to make a career switch

The goal: To sound credible and qualified

Kate Harris was a chemist and researcher who had spent ten years working in academia before deciding she needed to make a career switch. Uncertain of what career path to follow next, Kate enrolled in an executive MBA program to (hopefully) figure it out. During her first semester, Kate was amazed to find that she loved her finance classes. She had never taken an accounting or finance class before, nor did she think of herself a financier. Nonetheless, her logical mind and methodical thinking proved great assets in her finance class, and she found her peers came to her with questions about discounted cash flows and the time value of money.

Kate had envisioned working in a nonprofit or government as her next step after academia, but by the end of the semester she was convinced that finance should be her next move. Kate decided to combine her natural talents with her previous role in academia by focusing her job search on corporate finance departments in the healthcare industry.

After an on-campus presentation by Pfizer, Kate knew that it would be an ideal employer. She was simultaneously thrilled by the realization that she had cracked the nut of what she should do with her life, and nauseated by the prospect that she'd never get a job doing what she really wanted to do. She explained to a friend, "Why would Pfizer ever hire me? I don't know anything about the health-care industry, and I've never worked a day in finance. That seems like just too big of a leap for someone to take on me, don't you think?"

Finance was totally intuitive to Kate—it was just the way her mind worked. She was methodical, she was more comfortable with numbers and formulas than with lofty ideas, and she was good at taking ambiguity and breaking it into manageable pieces to find patterns.

Kate decided to just go with her gut and use her natural talents as the basis of her personal pitch instead of focusing on her previous experience (or lack thereof). Let's take a look at how Kate might have handled herself at a recruiting event.

The Strategy

1. The punch line: Your destination
2. The backstory: Think skills-based versus industry- or experience-based
3. Connect the dots: Why is this a logical next step?

Kate: Hello, my name is Kate Harris, and I'm at the executive MBA program at Rutgers.

Recruiter: Hi, Kate, nice to meet you. Thanks for coming to the Pfizer open house.

Kate:	My pleasure. I really enjoyed the overview of the company, and I'm very interested in potential opportunities with your corporate finance department. **[Punch Line: Destination]**
Recruiter:	Really, what's your background? Are you in the health-care industry now?
Kate:	Actually, I've been in academia for the last ten years working as a chemist and researcher, so, no, not exactly. **[Backstory]**
Recruiter:	Really? Why are you thinking about finance and not research and development, which would seem to make a lot of sense?
Kate:	Amazingly, finance is just completely intuitive to me and totally fascinating. It turns out that's just the way I'm wired. I loved my finance classes this semester, and I was amazed at how easy the concepts came to me. My thought processes work in much the same way, and I almost feel like it's a perfect match for my skill set and interests. **[Backstory and Connect the Dots]**
Recruiter:	Well, that's certainly interesting. We don't have many scientists who make the leap outside of R&D, but it's definitely worth continuing the conversation. I know there are people who'd be interested to hear your perspective on things.

Kate: That would be great. I'd love to speak with some of your colleagues. Do you have a card by chance?

Here's some additional example language Kate could have used at the recruiting event.

---

1. DESTINATION

- I'm a former chemist in the executive MBA program here at Rutgers, and I'm looking for a position in corporate finance.
- I really enjoyed the overview of the company, and I'm very interested in potential opportunities with your corporate finance department.
- I'm looking to move into corporate finance. I loved my finance classes this semester and realized that's what I want to do going forward.
- I'm a scientist who, it turns out, loves finance, and I'm hoping to find a health-care company to work for to combine my talents and interests.

---

2. BACKSTORY AND CONNECT THE DOTS

- I spent the last ten years working as a chemist and researcher at UC Berkeley, but I decided last year I wanted to make a career switch.

- Amazingly, finance is just completely intuitive to me and totally fascinating.
- It turns out that's just the way I'm wired. I loved my finance classes this semester and I was amazed at how easily the concepts came to me.
- My thought processes work in much the same way. I'm very methodical and logical and I almost feel like finance is a perfect match of my skill set and interests.

Kate was a logical, methodical thinker. She understood finance inherently. It's highly likely that someone in corporate finance in big pharma would take a chance on a smart and talented young woman who explained that she wanted to transition from chemistry to finance because that was how her brain worked.

Connecting the Dots

Connecting the dots seems to be the biggest challenge for people transitioning into new roles or looking to make the leap from one industry or organization to another.

Ethan, a retired trade-show executive, had recently joined a nonprofit board and had been asked to provide a brief bio to the board. He had planned on including his typical spiel—thirty years of experience building and running trade shows in North America.

The nonprofit had just lost its spiritual leader, was losing members faster than it was gaining new ones, and was going through an identity crisis of sorts. As Ethan thought about introducing himself to the board as the trade-show guy, he realized that snapshot didn't really do him justice. How did trade-show executive communicate the sense of value and purpose Ethan hoped to bring to the board? Why and how was it relevant?

As Ethan thought about his experience and background more deeply, he realized that what he had in fact done for thirty years of his career was build communities. He had brought buyers and sellers together, irrespective of the product or service being exchanged. What he could and would help this nonprofit do was rebuild their fractured community. His experience as a trade-show executive was actually directly relevant and transferable—he just needed to change his thinking around what it was he was skilled at.

Ethan explained, "I was so focused on 'recent' that I never took a step back to focus on 'relevant.' Once I did, I was able to connect the dots, and it was crystal clear that I've been building communities for the past thirty years." With his transformation in thinking from "trade-show exec" to "builder of communities," Ethan made his introduction to his new board in a way that resonated with colleagues and positioned him as the go-to guy to help meet the challenges of the organization.

Here are some phrases that may help you to connect the dots of *your* story.

CAREER SWITCHER

- I always knew I wanted to work for myself one day. I love the challenge of building something of my own, and I'm better at executing my own ideas than following other people's directives.
- I did like strategy consulting, but microfinance is so much more rewarding and fulfilling personally and I'm dying to become part of Grameen.
- I decided after being a starving artist for ten years that I want to help other artists by working for a foundation that funds the creative arts.
- I really enjoy retail, but I know I've got more creativity in me than I'm using. I'm looking to find a small design firm that will take a chance on an unknown.

ROLE SWITCHER

- Starwood's hotel management program was excellent, and I knew pretty quickly after my rotation in the restaurant that I wanted to be a chef.
- Media buying is challenging and rewarding, but I want to move into a more strategic corporate role at the company.
- I studied economics and always thought I'd end up in public policy, but humanitarian work drew me in after I spent a year with the United Nations.

- I enjoyed being an operations manager, but I'm interested in broadening my viewpoint and the general management rotation here is a great way to do that.

FIRM SWITCHER

- I enjoyed working at Expedia, but as the company grew, I wanted to go somewhere smaller and more entrepreneurial, and Kayak fit the bill.
- I spent seven great years with Kraft, but I'm excited about this new role at Hershey's, and I hope to add significant value given my operations background.
- I went from Oracle to Palm to Netflix and just kept following my mentor because he was brilliant and I loved working for him.
- Coming over to LinkedIn from CareerBuilder was a no-brainer. I'm excited to be a part of all the new innovations that LinkedIn is rolling out.

Here are some additional examples of what your destination language might sound like.

DESTINATION

- The next logical step seems to be . . .
- This job/role will be a great intersection of my previous experiences.
- I want to leverage my industry expertise by . . .
- My goal is to broaden my perspective.
- My goal is to really dig down and learn the operations of the organization.
- I'm hoping to get a bigger-picture view.
- I want to see firsthand how the manufacturing process works.

The Linear Career Path

Finally, what if you're not a Peace Corps volunteer turned investment banker or a classical-music major turned filmmaker? What if you studied elementary education as an undergrad and knew you wanted to be a teacher since you were eight years old? You spent your summers as a teaching assistant in the California public school system and now need to stand out among the hundreds of applicants applying for ten openings in the K–5 grades in your district.

What then? How does the elevator pitch impact you? In this case, it's not about connecting the dots—your career path is linear and makes all the sense in the world. Instead, you need to differentiate yourself from your peers and show what you bring to the table that is different, special, and memorable.

The personal pitch here is all about personalizing your story. Why have you always wanted to become a teacher? What is it that enables you to connect with students and leave them with a smile on their face and a desire to learn? Why do you stay in touch with students years after they've left your classroom? How did it come about that the curriculum you worked on with the superintendent of your school district is now being launched as a pilot program for other schools across the state?

The point is, you may have achievements, big or small, that set you apart from your peers. Or you may just have passion and enthusiasm that is real and contagious: people see the spark in your eye and they believe your story—they "get" why you want to be a teacher and why students feel compelled to do their best work for you.

In this case, the elevator pitch action strategy is the same as it is for the career switcher, but instead of talking about your transition and tying together your old and new experiences, you instead want to emphasize your key differentiator and show how or why you stand out from the pack.

The Strategy

1. Punch line
2. Backstory
3. Key differentiator

The example language behind the key differentiator will vary widely. However, consideration of a few broad categories may help to jump-start how you think about your unique talent:

- *A notable accomplishment*—publishing a research paper in college or playing the violin with the Philadelphia Orchestra as a child.
- *A unique or transformative experience*—studying abroad in Madrid as a college student or traveling to see the Panama Canal as a young adult.
- *A lifelong passion*—spending your summers as an intern on Capitol Hill and working for your state senator's reelection campaign.

For those of you who have followed a linear career path, the following example language should help you craft your personal pitch.

3. KEY DIFFERENTIATOR

- *Notable accomplishment:* I'm particularly proud of the reading-comprehension curriculum I worked on. It's being rolled out statewide by the district superintendent.
- *Unique/transformative experience:* Working as public health aid in Ecuador for six months forever changed my worldview and allows me to empathize with the patients in the hospital.
- *Lifelong passion:* I was a tech geek my whole life. I created a Web forum in college for student entrepreneurs, and it was an amazing learning experience. We had over twenty thousand users before it was acquired by a small firm in California.

- I've lived in Las Vegas my whole life and I've grown up surrounded by the gaming and hospitality industries. I can't figure out why no one is doing anything there with green building, so I'm going to fill in the gap.

TROUBLESHOOTING

Q: How can I improve my personal elevator pitch?

A: The only way to nail your personal pitch is to do your homework and practice. Think long and hard about your background and your goals. Understand what is unique and compelling about your story (or stories). Clearly identify your goals, then work on crafting your story to meet those goals. Talk to your friends, ask for advice, ask to practice with colleagues and see if you bore the pants off them, or if they're intrigued.

Q: To have a successful elevator pitch, do I need to launch into a monologue of all my professional accomplishments? Doesn't that sound silly and contrived?

A: The key is to have all of your professional accomplishments on the top of your mind, so that they're readily available for your pitch. What's the punch line? What is your backstory—the supporting facts and highlights? Know your stuff cold and be ready to go off-the-cuff as needed; be prepared to launch into a longer response if someone inquires further. The key is to have the monologue ready and then be able to pull in the relevant pieces or additional tidbits as needed.

Cheat Sheet

Chapter 1: Master the Hello and Good-Bye

Hello

1. Introduction
2. Purpose of Your Call
3. Key Question

Good-bye

1. Thank You
2. Forward Momentum

Chapter 2: The Foolproof Download

Download: Status Update

1. The Punch Line: Status Update
2. Key Facts / Supporting Highlights
3. Forward Momentum

Download: Persuasive Argument

1. The Punch Line: Make Your Case
2. Key Facts / Supporting Highlights
3. Forward Momentum

Download: Outstanding Information

1. The Punch Line: Status Update
2. Outstanding Items
3. Forward Momentum

Chapter 3: Be Strategically Proactive

- Learn
- Excel
- Assist
- Redirect
- Network

Multiple-Choice Strategy

1. Be Proactive
2. Offer to Do One of Two Specific Things

Chapter 4: Manage Expectations

Prioritize

1. Know Your To-Do List
2. Communicate Your Action Plan
3. Ask for Confirmation / Feedback

Manage Expectations

1. Ask for Timing / Expectations
2. Be Transparent About Your Workload
3. Propose Action Plan

Push Back

1. Highlight Issue / Problem
2. State Rationale
3. Propose a Solution

Chapter 5: Ask for Help

The Smart Ask

1. Be Proactive
2. Ask for Resources / Guidance
3. Request Feedback or Offer Milestones

The Smart Ask, Part II

1. Start with What You Know
2. State Your Intended Direction
3. Ask for Feedback / Confirmation

Chapter 6: Ask for Feedback

Phase I: The Preparation

1. Plant the Seed
2. Schedule the Conversation
3. Provide Specific Guidance (of What You're Looking For)

Phase II: The Conversation

1. Ask for Concrete Ways to Improve
2. Say Thank You
3. Wait, Digest, and Revisit

Chapter 7: Answer Questions (You Don't Know the Answers To)

Answer a Question . . .

1. Here's What I Know
2. Here's What I Don't Know
3. Here's How I'll Figure It Out

Chapter 8: Raise a Red Flag

Raise a Red Flag

1. Highlight the Issue
2. State the Rationale
3. Propose a Solution

Raise a Red Flag—Time Off

1. Highlight the Issue
2. Cover Your Bases
3. Get Buy-In

Chapter 9: Manage a Crisis

Missing a Deadline

1. Here's What's Been Completed
2. Here's What's Still Outstanding
3. Here's How I'll Finish the Task

Missing the Boat

1. Explain Your Approach
2. Acknowledge Feedback
3. Offer Revised Action Plan

Dropping the Ball

1. Apologize
2. State Your Rationale
3. Promise to Do It ASAP

Chapter 10: Your Personal Elevator Pitch

1. The Punch Line / Destination
2. The Backstory
3. Connect the Dots / Forward Momentum

Tear-Out Cheat Sheet

Chapter 1: Master the Hello and Good-Bye

Hello

1. Introduction
2. Purpose of Your Call
3. Key Question

Good-Bye

1. Thank You
2. Forward Momentum

Chapter 2: The Foolproof Download

Download: Status Update

1. The Punch Line: Status Update
2. Key Facts / Supporting Highlights
3. Forward Momentum

Download: Persuasive Argument

1. The Punch Line: Make Your Case
2. Key Facts / Supporting Highlights
3. Forward Momentum

Download: Outstanding Information

1. The Punch Line: Status Update
2. Outstanding Items
3. Forward Momentum

Chapter 3: Be Strategically Proactive

- Learn
- Excel
- Assist
- Redirect
- Network

Multiple-Choice Strategy

1. Be Proactive
2. Offer to Do One or Two Specific Things

Chapter 4: Manage Expectations

Prioritize

1. Know Your To-Do List
2. Communicate Your Action Plan
3. Ask for Confirmation/Feedback

Manage Expectations

1. Ask for Timing/Expectations
2. Be Transparent About Your Workload
3. Propose Action Plan

Push Back

1. Highlight Issue/Problem
2. State Rationale
3. Propose a Solution

Chapter 5: Ask for Help

The Smart Ask

1. Be Proactive
2. Ask for Resources/Guidance
3. Request Feedback or Offer Milestones

The Smart Ask, Part II

1. Start with What You Know
2. State Your Intended Direction
3. Ask for Feedback/Confirmation

Chapter 6: Ask for Feedback

Phase I: The Preparation

1. Plant the Seed
2. Schedule the Conversation
3. Provide Specific Guidance (of What You're Looking For)

Phase II: The Conversation

1. Ask for Concrete Ways to Improve
2. Say Thank You
3. Wait, Digest, and Revisit

Chapter 7: Answer Questions (You Don't Know the Answers To)

Answer a Question . . .

1. Here's What I Know
2. Here's What I Don't Know
3. Here's How I'll Figure It Out

Chapter 8: Raise a Red Flag

Raise a Red Flag

1. Highlight the Issue
2. State the Rationale
3. Propose a Solution

Raise a Red Flag—time off

1. Highlight the Issue
2. Cover Your Bases
3. Get Buy-In

Chapter 9: Manage a Crisis

Missing a Deadline

1. Here's What's Been Completed
2. Here's What's Still Outstanding
3. Here's How I'll Finish the Task

Missing the Boat

1. Your Approach/Rationale
2. Acknowledge Feedback
3. Revised Action Plan

Dropping the Ball

1. Apologize
2. State Your Rationale
3. Promise to Do It ASAP

Chapter 10: Your Personal Elevator Pitch

1. The Punch Line / Destination
2. The Backstory
3. Connect the Dots / Forward Momentum

Acknowledgments

I am grateful beyond measure to the many people who helped bring this book to life:

To my literary agent, Todd Shuster, thank you for your unwavering guidance and support throughout the process. You "got it" from the moment we spoke, and your faith in me has been a source of continuous comfort ever since. Thank you also to Rachel Sussman at Zachary Shuster Harmsworth for your superb editing and for getting the proposal across the finish line.

To Alyse Diamond at St. Martin's Press for your brilliant editing. This book is so much better because of you: Thank you for whipping it (and me) into shape. And for making it fun along the way. Thank you also to Steve Boldt, Meg Drislane, Nadea Mina, Sarah Goldstein, Lisa Senz, and Matthew Shear at SMP for your fantastic work.

To Kate Lee of ICM for your wise suggestion to perhaps build a business before writing a book. Thank you for being an unknowing force in bringing both this company and book to life. And thank you to Daniel Roth for the introduction.

To Richard Roberts for providing my Wall Street exit strategy, for being a matchmaker extraordinaire (I am forever grateful for Todd and Arti), and perhaps most important, for being *the* Great on the Job exemplar.

To Karin Ash, former director of the Career Management Center at the Johnson School at Cornell, for not only taking a risk on me and giving me my first opportunity to present to a business school audience, but for the innumerable introductions and glowing referrals you provided to your colleagues across the country.

To my b-school girls. Your collective brainpower, determination, enthusiasm, and humor have inspired me since the moment we met. Kerry, Eileen, Christina, Megan, Nicole, and Liz—I continually learn from each of you, and I love you all.

To my informal board of advisers, the entrepreneurs at IGC—you have each given me powerful examples of life after the nine-to-five grind. To Amy, Adelaide, Marissa, Alex, Eden, and Cari—I am continually energized watching you build your businesses. I loved going through year one of Great on the Job with the work/play/eat/dish routine we had going on.

And to the chairwomen of that board, Lisa Roth and Jillian Straus—where would I be without your wise counsel, brilliant editing, endless brainstorming, tough critiquing, successful pitch writing, helpful media training, generous contact sharing, and of course, friendship and love?

To my Chicago crew, thank you to Halee, Leslie, Rachel, and Suzanne for 118 years of collective friendship.

To Ruthie and Dennis, the best parents anyone could

ever inherit. And to Stephanie Stiefel for being so over-the-top generous and supportive always.

To my mom, a woman who has been described as growing friends the way others grow flowers. You are the definition of generosity of spirit—thank you for cheering me on through every step of the journey.

And finally, this book exists for one and only one reason—because of my husband, Eric, who sees things in this world that no one else sees. Thank you for conceiving of, believing in, and lobbying for this crazy idea that just may yet change the world. There is no greater joy than being your partner in love, life, and thought.

And to our two little buttons, Bella Grace and Arden Richard, for bringing more joy and happiness into our lives than anyone could ever hope for.

Index

Accenture, 95
action strategies
  when answering questions
    you don't know, xxiv, 147,
    149–51, 154–60, 163, 249,
    255
  when asking for feedback,
    xxvii, 121, 128–33,
    138–39, 248, 254
  when asking for help,
    100–102, 104–5, 108–13,
    248, 254
  in crisis management, xxii,
    xxvii, 185, 187–90, 191,
    193, 195, 198–99, 250, 256
  for elevator pitches, xxvii,
    214–16, 218, 220, 223–25,
    228–31, 234–40, 250, 256
  expectations, performance,
    and, xxvii, 72–93, 247,
    250, 253, 256
  GOTJ's use of, xi–xv, xix,
    xxv–xxvii
  for hello/good-bye
    communications, xxvi,
    12–15, 227, 245, 251
  for information delivery,
    xxiv, xxvi, 25–27, 31–32,
    33–35, 42, 246, 252
  when raising red flags, xxi,
    xxvii, 166–67, 169, 171–72,
    174–77, 178–82, 249, 255
  for time-off requests, 178–81,
    249, 255
answering questions (you don't
  know), x, 145
  cheat sheet guide to, 249,
    255
  excuses/disclaimers and, 149
  forward momentum and,
    xxiv, 149–51, 154–55,
    157–60, 163, 249, 255
  honesty/transparency in,
    xxviii, 149, 154, 157–58,
    160
  knowledge, demonstration
    of, when, 147–49, 150,
    152–53, 156–61, 249, 255
  proactive strategies/initiative
    in, xxiv, 147, 149–51,
    154–60, 163, 249, 255
  uncertainty and, 161–63